ONE TRIP TO KENYA

DAVID EDGREN

Nampa, Idaho | www.pacificpress.com

Cover design by Gerald Lee Monks
Cover design resources supplied by the author
Inside design by Aaron Troia

Copyright © 2019 by Pacific Press® Publishing Association
Printed in the United States of America
All rights reserved

The author assumes full responsibility for the accuracy of all facts and quotations as cited in this book.

Unless otherwise noted, Scripture quotations are from the Christian Standard Bible. Copyright © 2017 by Holman Bible Publishers. Used by permission. Christian Standard Bible®, and CSB® are federally registered trademarks of Holman Bible Publishers, all rights reserved.

Additional copies of this book are available for purchase by calling toll-free 1-800-765-6955 or by visiting http://www.adventistbookcenter.com.

Library of Congress Cataloging-in-Publication Data
Names: Edgren, David, 1972- author.
Title: One trip to Kenya / David Edgren.
Description: Nampa, Idaho : Pacific Press Publishing Association, [2019]
Identifiers: LCCN 2018045586 | ISBN 9780816364701 (pbk. : alk. paper)
Subjects: LCSH: Edgren, David, 1972—Diaries. | Missionaries—Kenya—Diaries. | Church work with the poor—Kenya—General Conference of Seventh-day Adventists.
Classification: LCC BV3625.K42 E34 2019 | DDC 266/.67092 [B] —dc23 LC record available at https://lccn.loc.gov/2018045586

January 2019

Table of Contents

Preface	Before Kenya	5
Introduction	Two Men	9
Chapter 1	Naming Poverty	11
Chapter 2	December 25: Ready to Depart	14
Chapter 3	The Brave Little Boy	18
Chapter 4	December 26: Bye-Bye Dubai	20
Chapter 5	Carole's Story	23
Chapter 6	December 27: The Worst Road in Kenya	27
Chapter 7	Angelo's Story	31
Chapter 8	December 28: Luke 15—Finding the Lost	37
Chapter 9	Joseph's Story	40
Chapter 10	December 29: The Maasai Life	47
Chapter 11	Maasai Cows	52
Chapter 12	December 30: Expect Anything in Kenya	58
Chapter 13	December 31: Opening Sabbath	61
Chapter 14	Vivian's Story	67
Chapter 15	December 31: Closing Sabbath	71
Chapter 16	January 3: Walk-Ins	75
Chapter 17	David's Story	79
Chapter 18	January 4: Leaving Kapune	83
Chapter 19	January 5: First-World Problems	86
Chapter 20	Nestor's Story	91
Chapter 21	January 6: Hands of Hope Academy	95
Chapter 22	Eucabeth's Story	101
Chapter 23	January 7: Sabbath at Hands of Hope Academy	104

Chapter 24	Sabbath Testimonies	107
Chapter 25	January 8: Sunday in Eldoret	113
Chapter 26	So Many Stories	117
Chapter 27	When the Lost Is Found	124

Preface

Before Kenya

I love children, and Africa is filled with children. I always knew that one day I would go to Africa, with my visit focusing on children. My dilemma was choosing where to go.

Nearly a year before the trip, in January 2016, Carole Platt contacted me on Facebook. I had met her some years before at a camp meeting in Brisbane, Australia, where I was telling Bible stories to the Juniors. Sometime later I discovered I had met her husband, Leon, at another camp meeting, this time in South Australia.

While I had been telling Bible stories to the kids, Carole and Leon had been telling stories about other children—the ones they help in their work with Education Care Projects—Kenya.

As Carole and I chatted, she began telling me about the two partner organizations in Kenya they were working with. These groups, with the full support of governmental authorities, rescued children from desperate situations. Most of the children were without parents and needed help in order to survive and have a chance of living happy and fulfilled lives. These rescued children were taken to a safe place, fed, clothed, and educated by people who love them and have their best interests at heart.

Carole asked me if I would like to go and tell Bible stories to the children; many of them have never heard how much God loves them. Now, there is nothing I love more than telling Bible stories—and no better audience than kids! So, of course, I said yes.

The rest of 2016 was filled with conversations and planning. I was to spend one week in Maasai land with the children rescued by Joseph Suyia Lekumok—all sixteen of them were at his home for the school

The four adventurers! David Edgren, Courtney Tyler, Carole and Leon Platt.

holidays—and one week at Hands of Hope Academy in the town of Mosoriot. The third week would be spent traveling between points, and two days would be filled with seeing the animals in the Maasai Mara National Reserve.

But the plan for the first week grew and grew. The original plan to tell stories from the Bible to children blossomed into preaching under a big tent. People walked for hours each morning to come to the revival meetings. Each day we had two meetings—one before lunch and one after lunch.

After the second meeting of the day, the travelers returned home. The children in the care of Joseph and Mercy, who were home for the Christmas holidays, stayed in the same mud hut as Leon, Carole, Courtney Tyler, a young woman also along on the trip, and myself. They were in their room filled with bunk beds, and we were in our private rooms. Each evening we had a time of worship and telling of Bible stories in the lounge room of our hut.

Many adventures filled this first week, and Joseph told me many tales of the children in his care. Some of those stories are recorded in this book, but many more were too painful and graphic to write.

The rest of the time in Kenya—the week at Hands of Hope Academy, my safari, and the road between these points—fill the rest of the pages of this book.

It is amazing how much can happen in three weeks!

Introduction

Two Men

Leon and Carole Platt have fallen deeply in love with the children of Kenya. During their visits, they have become dear friends with two Kenyan men who look after children—many of whom are orphans.

During the months of discussion about joining the Platts on a trip to Kenya, Carole began pouring stories into my heart through her keyboard. She told story after story of children being looked after by Joseph and Nestor, the two men who care for children in different areas of Kenya. Joseph, a country man, lives in a Maasai village. Nestor, a city man, lives in Mosoriot near the city of Eldoret. Both men have been called by God to rescue and care for children.

Carole recounted stories of the children rescued by Joseph and Nestor: some from homelessness and drug addiction near a garbage dump, some from sex slavery, some orphans, and some with parents who were unable or unwilling to care for them. All these children were in need of a safe place, education, and love.

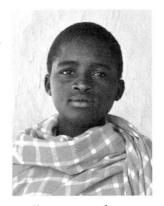

Sharon is one of many children living healthy, happy lives due to the work of Education Care Projects—Kenya.

The number of children helped grows each year as these two Christ-centered Seventh-day Adventist men search for, rescue, feed, educate, and love God's children in Kenya. All this is made possible by the belief and support of Carole, Leon, and their fundraising expertise through Education Care Projects—Kenya.

After telling me she organizes trips to Kenya for volunteers to see and help the children, Carole said, "You'd be great, David!"

"What would I do?" I asked. "I'm not very good with my hands, except on a QWERTY keyboard."

"Tell stories!" Carole said. "Most of these children have not heard about Jesus or the Bible. You could tell them stories. Do what you do so well!"

"In English? I don't speak their language."

"Some speak English," Carole said. "The rest are very comfortable listening to a translator. We use them all the time."

This is where my adventure began—with an idea and an invitation.

The plan solidified. I was to tell Bible stories to the children in both places, while Courtney presented talks to the young women and Leon and Carole busied themselves with other various projects already underway. Along with telling stories, I was to listen and learn the stories of Joseph and Nestor—the country man and the city man.

While in Kenya, I blogged much of what I learned and experienced; I wrote more than thirty thousand words in less than three weeks! When I returned home, I was to fashion those blogs into a book—this book. It was to be a travel journal of sorts, a compendium of stories, and a testimonial treasure trove.

And hopefully, upon reading this book, people will hear the desperate cries of the children of Kenya and be inspired to become involved.

So now we go to Africa in first person in real time.

Be blessed!

Chapter 1

Naming Poverty

Africa—one word with so many meanings: people, poverty, resources, dirt, wealth, war, safari, starvation, children, genocide, beauty, abuse, power, orphans.

Africa is home to every seventh person on Earth. Within its fifty-four countries, nearly two thousand languages are spoken; each represents a unique people group and a distinct culture.

Over the past few hundred years, these ancient cultures have been given a crash course in Western thought and morality. Along with education and modern medicine, Westerners have brought cultures and ideologies that changed Africa both for the better and for the worse.

Today, Africa is a country of extremes. Spiritual darkness and emotional devastation contrast with the joy-filled resilience of rescued children. Opencut mines and rubbish-strewn city streets deface the same landmass graced with beautiful, green rolling hills and open savannas filled with giraffes, lions, elephants, rhinoceroses, leopards, and buffalo.

In Africa, the West is seen as the big brother who could swoop in and save the day, if only he would. Imported via the internet and mass media, Western pop culture paints a picture of a reality that does not exist.

In the West, a starving African child serves as the proverbial picture in the dictionary to define the word *poverty*. "Eat your dinner," Western parents say. "There are children starving in Africa." Yet, in reality, many African families live happy, thriving lives.

Poverty, written about by a thousand charitable organizations, parallels with one word—*money*. The internet abounds with scams and legitimate claims coming out of Africa, and each seeks the elixir of Western life—money.

Having grown up in the west of the West, I am deeply indoctrinated into this money mind-set. In California, the land of Hollywood and Silicon Valley, I was raised believing I could do anything I set my mind on. Among my childhood peers, making one's first million was an all-too-common goal on the way to maturity.

My first foray into the big world of poverty was a ten-day mission trip to Honduras. Departing my private boarding school in California with a collection of Nike-clad classmates, I walked dusty roads lined with cardboard houses. The first week of our time was spent building an orphanage. The final few days were spent, eyes squinting through Nikon lenses, exploring the Copán ruins.

From that trip, two memories have remained with me. The first is holding a malnourished baby who died days after we returned home. A faded photo is imprinted in my mind. In the photo, our trip leader holds the baby, smiling and crying at the same time.

The second memory is of a barefoot boy who helped us on the jobsite. Each day he approached me and said something in the local language while pointing at my work boots. I would offer him my shoes, and he would shake his head and wave his hands back and forth. On our final day at the orphanage, a local pastor shared the need for lightweight shoes. I returned to my room—as did most of my classmates—and retrieved my walking shoes. Later that day, as we bundled into the bus, the boy approached me and pointed to my boots once again. They were now the only shoes I had with me. I saw the translator and called him over. He explained that the boy wanted the shoes I had worn the day I arrived. "He's never had shoes," the translator said. Finally understanding his request, I had to tell the boy those shoes had been given away that morning. His little face fell. For a week, he had tried so hard to get his message through, and while willing, I didn't understand the request.

All these years later I barely remember the world-famous archaeological ruins at Copán. I remember as if it were yesterday, however, the barefoot boy and the starving baby. The emotions I felt are still with me and bring tears to my eyes even now.

In the three decades since, I have only had a few opportunities to enter places of poverty. While attending university, I took a break and lived in the Marshall Islands, serving as a teacher. As an adult, I rode the train across Australia and drove to the Outback in Western Australia, where I told stories to aboriginal children.

On another mission trip during my university days, I met and married Jenny, an Australian, thus becoming an Australian citizen myself. After that, I stayed in Australia where I studied theology and worked for the Seventh-day Adventist Church for fifteen years. During that time, my wife and I had three Australian babies who are now (mostly) grown up.

During the past four years, I have spent my working days at government elementary schools where I serve as a chaplain to children, teachers, and parents. They have helped me to understand that poverty is bigger than just money. There's something both nearby and nebulous to it. Poverty is to be without; but without what?

It wasn't until my trip to Africa, recounted in this book, that I was able to put my growing understanding of poverty into words. Like all words in a living language, *poverty* is developing in meaning within all of us.

Each of us drags a tale of a thousand stories long past. Like me, you are the sum total of the stories in your life—not of the stories themselves, but of how you choose to tell them.

So come with me on a journey through Kenya, and perhaps you will discover new meaning in poverty, as I did.

Chapter 2

December 25: Ready to Depart

The day is finally here.* I think this is the only Christmas Day in my life when I've been more excited about the end of the day than the beginning!

We opened our presents last night in the German tradition of my wife Jenny's family, which the kids seem to prefer to waiting until the crack of dawn on Christmas morning. We've tried it both ways. I've got to say that we parents certainly prefer to sleep in on Christmas morning!

This morning, while the rest of the family put their Christmas gifts to use, I checked and rechecked my bags, particularly the weight of each. I got the weight to about sixty pounds between the two bags with exactly fifteen pounds in the carry-on. The two bags contain fifty-five pounds of kids' shirts, shorts, pants, hoodies, dresses, and more. Each bag has an illustrated children's Bible tucked in between the clothes. One of them also has my toiletries, sandals, and a notebook in which I will write notes as I interview people.

I can't wait to see the happy faces as the kids receive the clothes!

In the carry-on are eleven pounds of my clothes, iPad, Kindle, charger, cords, and a battery that can charge both the iPad and a phone at once. There are also two little bags lovingly prepared and gifted to me by my wonderful daughter, Rachael. One has healthy snacks. The other bag, labeled "For extreme cases of boredom," is filled with activities for my childish mind.

---

* Journal entry for Sunday, December 25, 2016.

December 25: Ready to Depart

Angelo and one of the older girls look at the children's picture Bible we brought over for Joseph's family and rescued children.

At about 1:00 p.m., we headed over to visit Grandma. After a wonderful Christmas lunch at Grandma's house, we went home, and I had a quick nap. (I had only slept for a few hours the previous night due to my excitement.) I checked all my bags again, and then the boys loaded them in the car.

After hugging everyone and saying farewell to my lads and lady, Jenny and I headed to the airport. Fifteen minutes later I returned home to retrieve my mobile phone, which was faithfully charging on the bedside table. An hour later Jenny and I said farewell to each other. Fifteen minutes after that, I returned to the curb to retrieve my mobile phone, which was faithfully charging in the dashboard console.

Half an hour later, as I was filling in my customs departure card, a security guard came in from the X-ray machines holding a phone and shouted, "Did anyone leave their phone at the security station?" I checked my pocket and retrieved my phone, which was resting where I always keep it. I said, loudly enough for the security person to look at me sternly and the guy next to me to snort to himself, "I've left my phone everywhere else today, until now!"

In the passport queue, the couple in front of me asked where I was going. I said, "Kenya, to tell stories to children at two schools!" They both smiled and said something about that being a nice thing. Then I asked, "Where are you going?" With a smile, the woman said, "Kenya as well."

"Oh!" I said, "What will you be doing?"

She looked guilty. "Just going on a safari."

"How long?" I asked.

"Three weeks," she said, and she looked a bit upset now. Her eyes said, *We're not doing anything for anyone else, just us.*

"That's cool," I said. "Have fun! I'm doing a two-day safari at the end of my three weeks. I'm really looking forward to it!"

Now I am sitting in a small café in the international departure area. The flight boards in forty-five minutes. I'm so glad for the opportunities I've been given in my life.

I've done a lot of selfish things in my life, usually because I believed they would make me happy. Sometimes they did. But those fleeting joys lasted little longer than the moments themselves.

And yet, it is always in the others-focused minutes and hours—and at rare blessed times, weeks—that I am reminded that the most meaningful moments in life are the ones that we give away.

The golden rule is bigger than a playground, a family, or a lifetime. When we humbly do for others what we would have them do for us (if we were in their situation), we change the world one playground, family, and life at a time for eternity.

That's what happened on the first Christmas, when the Creator of the universe put Himself in our shoes. He became one of us, walked among us, and gave us what we needed for eternity because He loved.

He still does. He loves you and me more than words can say, so He showed us—that's what love does when words are not enough.

Jesus reached into the muck of our lives and grabbed us tight. He dove into the muddy pit we were mired in, defeated the darkness, and pulled us up into His light.

Then ever so gently, Jesus wiped the crud out of our eyes so that we could see past ourselves, our playground, our family, and our lives. And He

December 25: Ready to Depart

gave us a new vision—one designed especially for us. But He doesn't stop there. He presents something worth seeing—Himself. And in beholding, we are changed into His likeness. Compelled by His love, we reach out to the world in the hopes of bringing another in from the darkness.

Living in the light, we see more clearly than before.

It's up to each of us to focus on that vision and follow it into the light of God's glory—and join the mission to change the world!

Chapter 3

The Brave Little Boy

"He was terrified of me," Carole said. She had tried everything—wrapping a Maasai skirt around herself, pulling her black sweater sleeves down to cover her skin, and even giving him a knitted sweater—but when Carole tried to go near the little boy, he cried out in fright.

"He had never seen a white person," Carole explained. "I did everything to show I was not a threat, but there was no hiding my face!"

Other people tried to help. The local Maasai leader, Joseph, came over and put his arm around Carole to show she was a friend. The boy's aunt held Carole's hand. Nothing would convince the boy.

"I so wanted to comfort him but I couldn't," Carole expressed. "I wonder if this is how God must feel at times."

The little boy had come with his auntie to enroll in the Enkishon Emaa Academy, which is a school being built in Kapune by Education Care Projects—Kenya. "He's on the waiting list now," Carole said. "His auntie is looking after nine kids. She has her six and her sister's three. Sadly, her husband just died."

Carole told me, "Finally, after his auntie held my hand, he let me touch his hand. Poor little darling." The brave little boy then accepted the sweater and stood outside for a photo of himself with his auntie.

"This ministry is about educating children," Carole continued, "but I also want them to learn about Jesus and come to Him. I want the boys to see a model of real Christian manhood and the girls to see Christian womanhood. That will change their lives. And it will change Maasai land as well. Joseph and his wife are wonderful role models!"

Reflecting on the little boy's struggles to accept her, Carole stated, "I guess that's why Jesus came in our likeness—so we would not be afraid of Him."

Chapter 4

December 26: Bye-Bye Dubai

I can't say I wasn't warned about Dubai.*

My mother-in-law likes to tell a story from my wife's childhood of the time the family stopped in Dubai while en route to Germany. It was a hot day, and in dire need of water, they made their way to a café and ordered a bottle of water. The host turned, filled an empty bottle with water, put a lid on it, and delivered it with the simple request, "Five dollars, please."

I was struck by the distinct difference offered today at the Dubai airport when, in the men's restroom, my every move—nearly—was assisted by a helpful attendant. As I headed toward a stall, I was compelled to wait and watch as the floor was quickly mopped and the toilet seat wiped with copious amounts of toilet paper furiously and dramatically drawn from the wall dispenser. Then I was invited in with a generous wave, as if a king were being announced as he approached his throne. Upon nearing the washbasin, my trusty assistant again appeared; this time to dutifully depress the soap dispenser so that I need not touch it as I washed my hands in the lukewarm tap water. Having a personal assistant in the restroom was an unexpected but not a completely unappreciated experience.

While the Dubai airport has improved and is not the kind of place that would sell you rebottled water as the café did, its prices have followed its service into the stratosphere. Approaching a café counter and ordering a

---

* Journal entry for Monday, December 26, 2016.

December 26: Bye-Bye Dubai

hot drink, I was told to sit. "We serve you!" the man said. "Then you pay when you finish." That should have been the first sign of the price to come.

Having just finished a fourteen-hour flight from Melbourne, I was looking forward to a large, warm drink rather than the small after-dinner cup I had received some hours earlier.

A few minutes after we sat down, we saw a waiter come to our table and I ordered the hot drink again. It was scribbled down on a notepad, as was Courtney's hot chocolate. Courtney had just completed the Brisbane–Dubai flight. We had met here and were on our way to help Education Care Projects—Kenya for the next three weeks.

With four hours to kill, we leisurely drank our drinks and chatted about our lives. Having never met before, we had plenty of material with which to fill the time.

When we finished, we approached the cashier and asked him to split the bill. I paid for my drink on my bank card and headed outside the crowded café to wait for Courtney. After some time, I grew concerned and returned. Courtney's card wasn't playing nice with their machine, and she had pulled out some American cash.

"We can only give you local currency as change," the man said. Courtney was not impressed as we were soon to leave Dubai and she had no need for local currency.

I handed the cashier my card again, and the ordeal was over. After we got outside the café, Courtney said, "He was going to charge me seven dollars and thirty cents American for that hot chocolate!"

I smiled and told Courtney the story of the five-dollar bottle of water from yesteryear. "Let's have a look at my account and see what it actually cost," I laughed.

Sitting at our gate, I loaded my phone's banking app and looked at the two drinks, now itemized due to the separate transactions. Courtney's cup of hot chocolate was a miserly $6.75 USD ($9.40 AUD), and my large, hot drink—a cool $8.17 USD ($11.38 AUD).

"That's one thing I love about travel," I said to Courtney. "There's an adventure around every corner!"

She laughed. "True!"

"From now on," I said, "I shall call Dubai the land of the eleven-dollar latte." A few hours later I sat cramped in the last row of the plane, less than an hour from Nairobi.

Bye-bye, Dubai.

Hello, Kenya!

Chapter 5

Carole's Story

Carole Platt has had a heart for Africa since her parents read the Jungle Doctor books to her when she was a preschooler. This series of books, written by Dr. Paul White, an Australian missionary, has titles such as *Monkey Tales, Hippo Happenings, Rhino Rumblings, Jungle Doctor's Africa*, and many more. Carole was transfixed while listening to the stories, both then and later on when reading them again and again for herself as she got older. Carole dreamed that one day she would be a nurse in a mission hospital in Africa. Instead, she became a teacher in her home country of Australia, but she had a lifelong fascination for Africa.

In 2007, Carole heard of an Adventist minister taking a group to visit an orphanage in Kenya. Finished raising her own children, Carole decided the time was right to head into the African adventure of her childhood dreams. Taking time off work, she joined the trip to an orphanage in Webuye in western Kenya.

"While we were there," Carole said, "I saw firsthand the plight of the orphans. AIDS had created hundreds of thousands of them, and it made a big impression on my mind."

Back in Australia, Carole could not settle back into life as usual. She had to do something to help. Along with two other Australians, she started a sponsorship program to help with the cost of educating the orphans they encountered during their time in Kenya.

Visiting the orphans again in 2010, Carole had an experience that helped to shape her current vision. While unexpectedly stranded in a Nairobi airport, she struck up a conversation with a Kenyan man who was also waiting. The man, an enthusiastic Baptist lay preacher and local tour operator, said something that frames Carole's passion and work in Kenya to this day.

Carole said, "He told us all Africa's children need is an opportunity."

Raised in Australia, Carole had been given every opportunity. The simple words of this man revealed the devastating difference between a childhood in Australia and one in Africa. Orphans in Kenya need someone to provide them with even the most basic opportunities. Education Care Projects—Kenya, Carole's sponsorship program, focuses on this one mission: creating opportunities for the children of Kenya.

Sometime after Carole and Leon started sponsoring the children they had visited, it became clear the funds were being mismanaged. They quickly stopped the funds and began the process of finding a trustworthy partner in Kenya.

A nurse friend of Carole's who had a Rotary Australia World Community Service project in Kenya offered to take her on his next trip. He said he would introduce her to his receiving Rotary Club in Nakuru. Having a sponsoring Rotary Club in Australia and a receiving club in Kenya seemed the best option for international accountability.

"I thought and prayed about it," Carole said, "but it just seemed too hard and too expensive."

About to give up, Carole had an experience that gave her clear direction. One afternoon, feeling particularly sad about the whole project, she decided to mow the lawn. She knew exercise was an effective way to lift a depressed spirit. As she mowed their lawn in Mullumbimby, New South Wales, Carole passed beneath their big bohemia tree and received a challenging message.

"I didn't hear an audible voice, but the thoughts came very clearly into my mind," Carole stated. *"Don't be a victim of your circumstances. Get up, and walk through the doors I am opening for you."*

After talking to her husband, Leon, Carole decided to go back to Kenya.

While in Kenya, she found that everything fell into place. Carole visited Joseph Suyia Lekumok in Kapune. Joseph and other concerned Maasai people had formed an nongovernmental organization (NGO) known as the Enkishon Emaa Welfare Organization. They had been praying for sponsors to help them rescue and educate children who had gone through awful trauma. Their prayers, unanswered for years, were now fulfilled.

"I first heard about Joseph and his wife, Mercy, when we stayed at a beautiful tourist lodge on the edge of the Maasai Mara game park called Mara West," Carole stated. "Rose, the manager at that time, told me about a group of Maasai concerned with the plight of orphaned children, especially young girls in danger of female genital mutilation and forced marriage."

Rose told Carole that Joseph's group had tried for years to raise money for a school, but it did not have the resources. Joseph was an honest man, Rose promised, and she recommended him and his work to Carole and her organization.

"When I finally met Joseph, he took Rose and me to a restaurant," Carole said. "I assumed he would expect me to buy lunch." Westerners are often believed to have unending access to money. Carole hadn't budgeted to buy food for herself and two other people. "When our meal was over," Carole said, "the waiter bought the bill to us. Before I could do anything, Joseph picked it up and said, 'Madam, allow me.' "

Carole laughed, "I could hardly believe it—a Kenyan was paying for my meal! I thought to myself, *This is a man I can trust.*"

Days later, the Rotary Club accepted Carole's project and signed the needed paperwork. "I even had the signature of Kenya's Rotary governor," Carole said.

Sitting on a plane, heading home from Nairobi, Carole considered all that had come to fruition. The challenge received under the bohemia tree in Mullumbimby had flowered into a bouquet of miracles in this single trip to Kenya. Working alongside Rotary Australia World Community Service, Education Care Projects—Kenya was formed, and accountability was assured in both Kenya and Australia. Carole had walked through the door God opened, and blessings followed.

Shortly after she returned to Australia, she was presented with another potential project in Kenya. Colin Hone, the Australian leader of Holy Spirit Ministries, told Carole he had just held meetings in Kenya. He told her about a young Rwandan man named Nestor who had a community-based organization called Hands of Hope East Africa.

Nestor's vision was to give street children an education and a safe place to live, thus setting them free from a lifelong cycle of poverty. Nestor had managed a project for Holy Spirit Ministries in Kenya, had handled all the money, and at the end, had returned it all safely and accounted for.

"When I heard this from Colin," Carole said, "I knew this was another man I could trust and work with in Kenya."

The Hands of Hope East Africa in Mosoriot, the Enkishon Emaa Welfare Organization in Kapune, and the Education Care Projects—Kenya in Australia now work together to provide opportunities for orphaned, abandoned, and underprivileged children and young adults in Kenya.

Chapter 6

December 27:
The Worst Road in Kenya

The journey from Nairobi to Kapune was invigorating, terrifying, and wonder-inducing.*

The beginning of the day was filled with unruly roundabouts. Each one presents its own challenge. The only similarity between this roundabout and the next one is the complete lack of rules as to how they are to be navigated.

Yield to traffic coming from the right? What's that? It's not a rule known in Kenya.

The bigger your vehicle, the more likely you'll get through the roundabout unscathed, unless you're riding one of the million-plus motorcycles in the city. If that's you, just weave in and out and around, over and under any potential setback, be it a parked vehicle with people huddled around its exposed smoking engine or a transport vehicle barreling through the roundabout using all the lanes. Just hang on, shut your eyes, and ride like you'll live another day, and you just might.

Before leaving Nairobi, Leon pulled over at a gas station, explaining, "I accidentally left a few liters of oil here. I purchased it yesterday before picking you up at the airport but forgot to take it." Not wanting to be late picking us up, Leon had decided to stop on the way out of town to pick it up today intead of yesterday.

As we pulled into the crowded gas station, the manager came rushing

---

* Journal entry for Tuesday, December 27, 2016.

out to our Toyota Prado and approached the driver's side window before Leon could even get out. Leon opened the door to the words, "You left your oil. I have it in the shop, waiting for you."

Leon got out and followed the man into the shop. A few minutes later, with the oil stored in the back, Leon took off once again. "Kenya has a lot of people who want to take you for a ride," Leon said, "The *mzungu* is a big target to the dishonest person. But time after time, we meet the good ones. I thanked him for being a godly man. He told me he believes in God and tries to do the right thing by all people."

"*Mzungu?*" I asked.

Leon laughed. "The white man. That's what they call us—*mzungu*."

We drove in silence for some time. We passed carts loaded high with wheat, charcoal, and other products. Each cart was ridden by one or two men and pulled by anywhere from one to three donkeys. The road was littered with speed bumps; originally built to slow people down, they had become the best place for one roadside shop after the next. Each shop carried just one or two products.

The bumps are so steep that the vehicle nearly comes to a stop at each one—unless you don't notice one, and then you are launched into the ceiling as a reminder to keep a wary eye for the next one. So the roadside shops are a welcome reminder: slow down, because speed kills—or gives you a massive headache, at the least.

Later, descending along the side of a large escarpment, Leon said, "That's the Great Rift Valley."

The mountain dropped away dramatically on the left (passenger) side of the vehicle, and I stared out into the abyss of ancient Africa. The chasm between rolling hills and occasional mounds gave evidence of prehistoric volcanic action. Leon pulled over and said, "We'll stop here for a look. They will try to sell you things. You can buy if you wish."

Stepping out of the vehicle, the ground fell away just a few meters away. A rickety wooden overlook made from pieces of old, rough-hewn timber invited the brave traveler to step out in faith. I could see through the overlook's many large cracks to the plummeting depths below.

Finally, I dared the few steps required to get out to the railing just to

December 27: The Worst Road in Kenya

prove to myself that I was a manly man. Proof gained, I retreated hastily to solid ground and leaned in a manly fashion against the bull bar of our rugged Toyota Prado. The Prado and I were a tough, brave pair, waiting patiently for the rest of the group. I was guarding the Prado, and it was defining me—a silent statement of solidarity and security in numbers.

While holding the bull bar in place, I was approached by a man with a basket of trinkets and treasures. He kept handing me things and speaking in broken English. "Just five hundred shillings," he said with each trinket he handed me. I dutifully took everything handed to me. When I had four of the big five made from petrified wood, my new salesman friend pulled out a paper bag and offered to package my purchase for me.

I had said several polite things during the interaction, all in an attempt to imply I was not purchasing today. Finally, as the bag was being filled, I said, "I don't want to buy anything."

The man looked shocked, took the trinkets from my hand, and said in his best English yet, "Fine!" Dropping the trinkets into his basket, he shuffled away to the next unwilling customer.

Back in the car, we began comparing currencies. Everything is in Kenya shillings (KSh) and after doing some crazy hard math (to my word-centric mind), we realized that one shilling is equivalent to one US cent. Those trinkets cost nearly five American dollars each.

When we reached the next big town, we pulled over to buy food supplies, eat lunch, and purchase SIM cards for our phones. We waited for a good forty-five minutes before it was our turn. We were amazed when we walked out of the Safaricom shop with three gigs of data and fifty minutes of talk time, having spent only thirteen US dollars!

Mobile technology has transformed the interconnectivity of the Kenyan people. With one simple tower on the occasional hill, mobile technology reaches even the most remote spot. There we were, two hours from the nearest paved road, and I was posting pictures, videos, and blog posts with four bars of 3G internet. Joseph said, "Yes, we are not remote Maasai; we are modern Maasai!"

As we passed through towns during the final leg of our journey, we made some speed bump stops to purchase local produce: a bag of tomatoes for

200 shillings, a bag of peas for 150 shillings, spring onions for 100 shillings, and potatoes for 350 shillings. Nothing seems to make the shopkeepers happier than selling to an *mzungu*. They laughed at every word from my mouth and expression of my face. They pretended to not understand "no," and it made for great opportunities to overdramatize the word *no*! I had fun, but I think they had more fun than I as they pushed their hands into the window filled with vegetables and said, "You take! You like!"

Traveling down a straight stretch of paved road, Leon said, "Here it comes. The worst road in Kenya, but it's the only way into Kapune." He turned right off the paved road and followed a rough stony road that had smooth spots on one shoulder where it was worn down by foot traffic and motorcycles. Each time we would encounter someone on that smooth path, the Prado would shimmy and shake as both wheels bumped out onto the stone-strewn road.

After some time, this road got worse. Huge ruts needed to be navigated. Large boulders blocked parts of the road and shoulders. Reaching yet another small village along the road, Leon turned sharply up a hill between two buildings. It was hard to call it a road at all.

What had been the worst road in Kenya now transformed into the best four-wheel-drive track in Kenya. It was steep, sideways, and had sharp corners, buildings, and people to avoid.

Finally, we came to a closed fence. Children materialized from the bushes all around. One boy opened the gate, and Leon said, "Here's the school we are building." It was just a foundation and the first few layers of concrete blocks, but the plan for the school was very easy to see: two classrooms, back to back, with doors at each end and chalkboards in the middle.

To finish our journey, Leon drove us the rest of the way—another ten minutes—to the village where Joseph Suyia Lekumok lives with his wife, Mercy, their five children, and the fifteen children they have rescued.

Chapter 7

Angelo's Story

In past generations, Angelo would have been killed at birth. At the time of his mother's marriage, she was unaware that she was pregnant by another man. This baby was considered cursed and would bring that curse upon his family. While most tribal Africans no longer murder babies born to such mothers, the stigma remains. These babies are still called "cursed."

Angelo's stepfather and his tribe still practice the old ways. Shamed by the birth of this cursed child, the stepfather decided to end the baby's life.

There are two ways death can be carried out. The first way is to lay the newborn infant on the threshold of a cow pen. The opening to the pen is only wide enough for one cow at a time. Then the cows are whipped into a frenzy and are forced to leave the pen. In their stressed state, the cows will panic and trample the baby in their effort to get out of the pen.

The second traditional way to kill a cursed child is by using poison. There is a long history in the Maasai culture of specially trained midwives who help in the delivery of babies. The Maasai men wait outside the hut as the baby is born while the women assist. The midwives are trained in the use of medicines. They have medicines that help life and medicines that end life, if needed. A curse was one of the reasons for ending the life of a baby.

Angelo's father paid the midwife who assisted in the birth to poison the baby. Because Angelo's mother didn't practice the old ways, the poisoning was done without her knowledge.

The poison entered the newborn's bloodstream and began its evil work. Amazingly, Angelo didn't die, but the poison damaged the little boy's mind. He would often drop into unconsciousness and have seizures that caused his little body to shake uncontrollably. Angelo's mother looked for a way out of the weight of having a cursed baby who had fits and was inconsolable. To protect the baby and herself, she sent little Angelo to live with her older brother's family.

Angelo's uncle kept him for a year and then sold him to a rich man who said he would help Angelo. Instead, Angelo was left outside with the animals. Angelo spent the next four years of his life, until he was five years old, living and eating with the rich man's livestock.

Maasai boys often look after the livestock. The rich man had sons but had sent them off to a private boarding school. Because he lived in a secluded place with his own water source and grazing area, the rich man did not fear other Maasai children seeing the boy at watering holes or in the fields. Angelo was alone with the animals and had occasional interactions with the rich man's family.

It was the only life Angelo knew.

Joseph has a network of informants he calls "ladies in the ground" who subtly infiltrate suspected situations. Mobile phones have made these types of rescues easier. Stories spread quickly, and when they reach Joseph's informers, they call him.

Upon hearing the story of Angelo, Joseph went to the site to see if the story was true. Getting to the boy was not easy. Joseph had to walk in at night to avoid the attention of the rich man. Then he had to find the boy.

The place where the rich man lived, like many Maasai homes, had no roads. The Maasai are great walkers. They will walk amazing distances and think nothing of it. Scientists have studied the Maasai people's metabolism and circulatory systems and are convinced that the generations of Maasai herders who walk all day long for their entire lives have made them a truly unique people. They walk faster and farther than most other people groups could even imagine.

Joseph decided he would need to walk through the jungle to get to little Angelo undetected. This meant he would be walking through the territory of lions, cheetahs, and elephants. So as he entered the jungle, Joseph found a tower (group) of giraffes and encouraged the animals to head in the direction he needed to go. Maasai have long used giraffes as their guides at night in dangerous areas. A giraffe will not knowingly walk near dangerous animals. For the entire twenty-nine-mile journey, Joseph shepherded the tower of giraffe as they smelled their way through the jungle, and he arrived safely on the other side well before morning.

After searching for some time from the edge of the jungle, Joseph found the boy alone, hiding in a bush, watching the rich man's cows. The boy was terrified of Joseph, having seen very few people in his life, and would not come out of the bush. Joseph noticed that the boy was wild and difficult to communicate with.

* * * * *

Convinced the story was true, Joseph used the weapon of his trade, a mobile phone, to call Leon and Carole Platt in Australia. If funds were not available, it would not be possible to provide for the boy.

Early in his rescue work, Joseph used to attempt to care for children on his own until funding could be found for putting the child into boarding school—the safest place in Kenya for threatened children. But now, well known for his work, Joseph cannot afford to take every child home to join his family of five children.

"I receive a call about a child in need of rescue nearly every day," Joseph told me. "I have fifteen children in the program right now. They are fully sponsored to go to school. They have food, clothes, education, and most important, they are safe."

Joseph paused and then asked, "Do you want to know how many children are on my list right now? Children that I have verified their stories and they need safety?"

"How many?" I asked.

"One hundred and sixty-one—that many need the safety of the program." Joseph studied me with his powerful Maasai stare. "Can you help us to help these children, David? Is this something you can do?"

"I will try, Joseph," I said with tears in my eyes. "I will tell your story. When Western people have their hearts touched, they are very loving, kind, and generous people. But in the West, everyone is asking for money.

So we need to hear real stories to believe the money will actually help."

"Thank you, David. Thank you so much!"

* * * * *

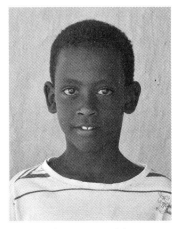

Angelo was rescued from a life of slavery and abuse. He is now an excellent student!

Joseph continued the story of little five-year-old Angelo.

After receiving the call about this urgent rescue, Leon and Carole added little Angelo to the prayer chain at Kingscliff Seventh-day Adventist Church, and within hours, offers to assist financially were made available.

They called Joseph back, and he went into action.

Joseph approached the boy and said, "I want to make you free and take you to a safe place, if you wish to come."

Angelo said, "I am free here. I suck milk from the cows whenever I want. I eat berries off any bush I want."

"His words were not good like this," Joseph said. "But he told me these things. He only knew one life. He had no idea how a child should be living."

Joseph made his way back out of the jungle and stayed in a nearby town. Every day he would talk to his "ladies in the ground" about how he should approach the boy, and numerous times he made the trip back through the jungle to visit the wild boy.

Finally, after two weeks of talking to Angelo, trust was built. He was convinced by Joseph's stories of a better life where children have food, clothing, education, and safety. Angelo agreed to come with Joseph.

Joseph took Angelo to a Catholic boarding school, which was the safest school in Maasai land. He paid for clothes, tuition, and food. Angelo had never worn shoes, never used toilet paper, and never brushed his teeth.

A few weeks later a call came from the school: "This boy is not able to be here. He bites the other children. He doesn't sit still to learn."

Joseph went to school with Angelo. He sat with him every day all day for many days. He helped Angelo do the right thing. He explained how to be a good student and play nice.

"This is why we need the school Leon is building," Joseph said. "It will be a safe place for children like Angelo. These children are struggling, so they need to be safe for a long time before they can be educated like normal children."

The little school is being built just over the hill from Joseph's land in Kapune, Kenya. Leon, a builder by trade, has been leading a team of eager locals to build the school.

Joseph stated, "When the Enkishon Emaa Academy is ready, we will take the children there. Most schools are after performance. We are about life."

Joseph talks a lot about justice. "I hear these stories," he said. "I see the men who are harming these children. And I want justice." Joseph paused to choose his words. "But I do not do justice. God does. I do charity. Kindness and safety are what I do. Justice is impossible in Kenya, but charity is possible."

Joseph uses the word *charity* where you and I would use the word *mercy*. There are a couple of reasons for this. First, it truly takes the charity of people like you and me to make Joseph's work possible. Second, the word *mercy* is reserved for one person in Joseph's life—one

Joseph and Mercy have five children of their own and care for nearly 20 more whom Joseph has rescued.

person who makes his work, his passion, and his heart for children possible. Mercy is the name of Joseph's wife.

I jokingly told Joseph that he should change his name to Justice. Then there could be Justice and Mercy working together in Kenya. He laughed and said, "No. Mercy is enough. Mercy is what the children need. I cannot bring justice. Only mercy."[1]

---

1. If you would like to help bring mercy to children like Angelo, please consider partnering with Education Care Projects—Kenya. Every dollar raised goes to the work in Kenya. There is no costly organization taking a cut. It's just Carole and Leon Platt and their partners donating their time and energy; and in Kapune, Joseph and Mercy are changing the world one child at a time.

Chapter 8

December 28:
Luke 15—Finding the Lost

After arriving and setting up our rooms, we had a light dinner.* Sitting in our kitchen next to smoldering charcoals with a pot of water coming to a boil, we ate toast with peanut butter and mashed bananas. Two pieces of toast and a few apple slices were all it took to satisfy my time-confused mind and body.

By the time the locals wandered into our mud-hut lounge, it was nearly 9:00 p.m. local time. Courtney and I were lost somewhere between there and the next morning soon to be dawning in Australia.

But what happened next was worth staying up for. The fifteen or so children who filled the room began to sing, led by Leon. The children who had entered so quietly now sang with joy. Then came the action songs. It was beautiful to watch and a lot of fun to join in. These kids have made an art of singing and laughing at the same time. If there were a picture next to the word *joy* in the dictionary, it would be a picture of these kids.

Leon said an opening prayer, and Joseph introduced me. Then we began exploring three stories that Jesus told about people finding things they had lost. Joseph translated for me.

"Have you ever lost something that you really needed?" I asked.

I have never told the stories in Luke 15 in a place where they made more sense. A shepherd loses one of his one hundred sheep and leaves the

---

* Journal entry for Wednesday, December 28, 2016.

ninety-nine in an open field while he searches and finds the lost one. The Maasai are shepherds. On our journey today, we drove past hundreds of sheep and goats being cared for by Maasai boys. And now, we were in a room filled with Maasai children.

"Have you ever helped look after the sheep or goats?" I asked and raised my hand. "Raise your hand if you have helped shepherd the animals." Hands went up around the room.

"This first story Jesus told, to show how much God loves each of you, was about a shepherd boy who lost one sheep. He counted one, two, three, four, five, . . . ninety-eight, ninety-nine. Oh no! One is missing! He counted again one, two, three, four, five, . . . ninety-eight, ninety-nine. Oh *no*! One sheep really was lost!"

Storyteller side note: This illustration worked really well alongside a translator. As Joseph translated the "one, two, three, four, five" it gave a sense of time passing so that the "ninety-eight, ninety-nine" seemed to be finishing the long effort of counting the sheep.

Wealth in Maasai land is based on the livestock you own. Maasai boys do not own the animals they shepherd. Losing an animal in your care would be a very stressful thing, indeed, and could even result in losing your job or worse.

So Jesus' first "lost" story spoke deeply to these children and to Joseph as he translated. Later, when I was down at the animal pen taking photos in the morning light, Joseph walked up to me. I told him this was the most meaningful place I had ever told the story about the lost sheep. He said, "Yes, it is very meaningful, most meaningful to us."

When I told the children that the boy found the sheep, put it on his shoulders, and took it back to the flock, there was a sense of relief around the room. My understanding of this story escalated even more as I told them that the shepherd had a party that night because he was so happy. All the children and adults nodded and smiled. They, too, have had such parties of joy!

Jesus' next two "lost" stories were received with as much agreement and understanding: A house turned over by a woman looking for one lost coin: every coin is precious to these people as money is hard to come by. A

December 28: Luke 15—Finding the Lost

son who takes his father's wealth and squanders it in the city: the city of Nairobi is a very real temptation to the country-born Maasai until they, too, have been destroyed by its temptations and come home broken. But to me, it was the first story that struck home.

Jesus knew the people He was talking to. And His stories still speak. A point that stood out to me was the importance of the party after finding what had been lost. There is true joy represented in these stories, especially to people in cultures similar to the one Jesus lived in.

As I reflect and write this, dapples of early morning light decorate the mud floor of our hut, built by the hands of the people whom we've come to serve. Reading Luke 15 once again, I smile at the beginning of the chapter. Jesus was telling these stories to answer an accusation made against Him by rich people. The Pharisees, often disconnected from the poverty and need in the world around them, were more concerned with their own reputation than the needs of others. They were concerned as they watched Jesus from afar: "All the tax collectors and sinners were approaching to listen to him. And the Pharisees and scribes were complaining, 'This man welcomes sinners and eats with them' " (Luke 15:1, 2)!

Jesus' series of stories answered the Pharisees' accusations: "I've got reason to party! Look at them coming to God!" But He did it by telling stories to the poor people sitting at His feet, stories they understood.

Then He finished the set of stories in a way that only the Pharisees would understand. Jesus challenged the rich and righteous men who had accused Him by revealing the true nature of the lost son's brother who, though he had lived with and worked for his father since he was a child, misunderstood his father's love completely. " 'Son,' he said to him, 'you are always with me, and everything I have is yours. But we had to celebrate and rejoice, because this brother of yours was dead and is alive again; he was lost and is found' " (Luke 15:31, 32).

Chapter 9

Joseph's Story

Joseph was the oldest of ten children in his mother's house. His father had two houses and two wives. The other wife had twelve children.

Because of the number of children his father had to support, the family was very poor. Education was a big challenge, but Joseph stayed in school and finished high school when he was eighteen years old. These were not easy times for him. To earn a little money, he would go out at night with his friends, chop trees down, and make charcoal. While the government is against charcoal manufacturing in this way, it is a customary practice, and many of the poorest of the poor make the little money they have in this way.

In Maasai land, we cooked our meals and boiled water for hot drinks and dishwater on top of pots filled with smoldering charcoal. It is the primary way to create an indoor heat source for cooking.

One night, as Joseph was chopping a tree down, he fainted. When he woke up, he was in the hospital. Joseph said, "They told me I needed to eat more if I planned to work so hard. They said, 'Joseph, you are starving.' "

When Joseph finished high school, his father told him there was no money for college and that he would have to go into the military. The military provides regular pay, prestige, and a lifetime plan of wealth and job security. "I refused," Joseph explained. "I wanted to do something to change the lives of people. If I go to the military, I will fight and become rich, but whose life will I change?" Joseph paused and looked up at me. "Helping people—this is my calling."

"Since I was young, I always liked helping people," Joseph stated. "I have always wanted to see justice for others. Poverty is a challenge. I knew

I wanted to help those without family and those who are destitute, like the widow and orphan."

Joseph struggled for a couple of years after high school before deciding to go to Nairobi to help people. A politician he had met in town one day had told him, "You come to Nairobi with a thousand shillings, and I will give you a job." Joseph hoped that once he was in the city, he would be able to help destitute people.

When he got to Nairobi, the politician took the thousand shillings and said, "Sit here in the hotel until I return. I will go get you a job."

Joseph said, "I sat there all day. He never came back." As it began to get dark, the hotel manager told Joseph he could not sit there anymore.

"I told them I was waiting for the politician. I refused to leave. They called the security guard in from the street to make me leave.

"It is a disgrace for a Maasai man to be grabbed and moved," Joseph said. "I told the soldier, 'Don't touch me, I will come.' " As Joseph followed the security guard out of the hotel, he was angry and frustrated. "I started to pray out loud to God in the Maasai language," Joseph said. "I was asking God why this happened to me."

When they got outside, the guard turned to Joseph and said, "I understand Maasai. Tell me what has happened to you." Joseph told him the entire story, and the guard said, "Stay by the door until 10:00 P.M., then I will be back for you."

During the night, a street patrol of two police officers came past and thought Joseph was a loitering homeless person. They did not believe his story and handcuffed him, intending to take him to jail for the night. Joseph begged them not to and told his story with such passion that they believed him, uncuffed him, and let him stay.

At 10:00 P.M., the security guard returned. He fed Joseph and led him to an empty room in the hotel. "Brother," he said, "you sleep here until 4:00 A.M. Then I will come and fix the room to look like you have not been here. If we get caught, I will have to pay for your stay. I cannot afford this."

Joseph stated, "This was my first time ever in a nice hotel. It was so nice!" At 4:00 A.M., Joseph rose. The guard, who was also the night manager, came and removed the sheets and prepared the room.

As Joseph walked down to the lobby, the morning desk person assumed he was a guest of the hotel and told him breakfast was ready. "They fed me until I was very full!"

That day Joseph looked for a job. He knew that Indian men had the biggest shops, so he went looking for Indian-owned stores and asked for a job. In the fifth shop, a lady was running the shop. She wanted to hire him, but when her husband returned, he tried to scare Joseph away by telling him it was very hard work. They decided to employ him as an industrial worker.

Although Joseph had a job, he had no place to sleep, no money, and no pay for one month. They fed the workers once a day with a meal of beans and maize.

"Life was a real challenge," Joseph explained. "I had no friend, no money. I started living like a street child, even though I knew I was not a street child. I slept on the back of parked trucks. It was so cold that some mornings I would push ice off my clothes. I was promised six thousand shillings a month, but each month I was given just three hundred shillings [three US dollars]."

To make enough money to survive, he and other factory workers would use their time off to sit in a *matatu*—a bus with fourteen seats—and make it look half full. This would get other people to believe the bus would leave soon. As the bus would fill, Joseph and his friends would get out one by one to make room. The matatu driver would slyly give them ten shillings as they exited. Once he had thirty shillings, he would buy soap and roasted maize (corncob) or potatoes to eat. Then he would go to the river, wash himself and his clothes with the soap, and go back to work.

"During this year," Joseph said, "I was crying to God to get me out of poverty. I had come to change people's lives in the city, and now I was a street child.

"Some nights while sleeping with the other street children on the trucks or in hidden areas, the police would wake us and force us to leave or take us to jail. Sometimes other boys would mistreat you, abuse you. The life was so tough."

After one year, Joseph's Indian boss said he trusted Joseph and made him his agent. As an agent, Joseph was responsible to do three things:

1. Go to the bank and get in the queue. When the time came for a signature, he used the man's mobile phone to call him and say, "Come sign."
2. Go to the tax department and get in the queue. When the time came for a signature, he would call the boss.
3. Go to the post office or airport to collect the mail or post things that needed to be sent.

Joseph was also given a storeroom in the man's factory in which to sleep.

After doing these three things each day for many weeks, he met a Maasai man in the tax department. The man asked Joseph why he was in the line every day. He explained he was an agent waiting in line. The other Maasai man said not to wait in line. "From now on," he said, "come straight to me, and I will do the papers." The Maasai man was one of the primary tax agents.

It didn't take the Indian man long to notice that Joseph had a direct line at the tax department. He told other Indian business owners, and they started using Joseph as well. "I was paid two hundred shillings per queue," Joseph said. "I was making six hundred shillings a day visiting the tax department for three Indian men."

Joseph could now afford his own small bedroom in which to live.

One day on an airport run, Joseph saw an *mzungu* woman crying. He asked her what was wrong. She said, "I'm absolutely finished." The woman's husband came over and explained they had come to Africa as missionaries to drill wells to provide water for tribes. They had been waiting for two weeks for the expensive drilling machine to pass through customs. They had decided the machines had been stolen. It is not unusual for imports to be stolen and sold when they come into the country.

Joseph said, "Don't leave. Let me see what I can do."

"The immigration minister was a Maasai Seventh-day Adventist man from my region," Joseph explained. "I knew this, but I did not know him. I knew his family were friends with my pastor. I called the pastor and asked him to convince the minister to help these people do God's work in Africa. The water from these wells would come to our people."

Twenty minutes later Joseph's phone rang. It was the immigration minister. "I am sending a vehicle for the three of you. Get in, and it will bring you to me."

"I told the *mzungu* man we were going to see the minister of immigration," Joseph said. "He did not believe me, but his wife convinced him. She said, 'We have no alternative. We must trust this boy.' "

When they reached the minister, he asked Joseph to come in alone with the customs papers. Once Joseph had explained the situation to the minister, things happened quickly. The minister picked up his phone and called the principal immigration officer to come to his office immediately.

When the man arrived, the minister asked him a question: "Who is the minister of immigration? If you think you are the minister, I will resign right now!" The other man was terrified and sweating. "If I am the minister, I need these things right now," said the minister, handing the officer the import papers.

"Give me three hours," the immigration officer said. "After that you can fire me or do whatever you wish."

"Your request is well granted!"

The officer left quickly.

The immigration minister said, "Go wait with the *mzungus*."

They paid for Joseph to stay the night in the same lodge as they did. The next morning the minister called and said, "I am sending you a car. Take it to the airport and see if the package has arrived."

When they arrived, the driver took them to the VIP section of the airport. When they got to the customs desk, they found that everything was there. The immigration officer had pulled out all the stops to ensure he kept his job: No customs duty was charged. The missionaries did not have to pay the value-added tax (VAT) for further purchases. This meant that anything these missionaries purchased during their entire stay there would have no government tax charged, and governmental transportation for both the missionaries and the bore drill was provided for any destination where they wished to go.

At the hotel, the missionaries asked Joseph what they could do for him in return.

"I want you to do two things," Joseph stated. "I want you to give thanks to God. He made all this happen. I want you to give thanks to the minister. If you will do those two things for me, I will be blessed."

They insisted on doing something for Joseph. For three days, they called him every afternoon and asked to meet him. They would buy lunch and ask again, "What can we do for you?"

"I stood by my principles," Joseph said.

They asked, "We will decide what to give to God. But we do not know what to give the minister in thanks. Please tell us what to give him."

"Give the minister textbooks for schoolchildren, and he will give them to the children of Kenya," Joseph said "You will have helped the children and made the minister look very good."

They went together to Macmillan Publishing in Nairobi. They explained they were missionaries from America and wanted to buy schoolbooks for children in Kenya.

That couple purchased seven hundred thousand shillings' worth of books and delivered them to the minister in seven Nissan minibuses.

The minister was so happy that he wanted to give them a present. They explained he had already given them back their ministry in Kenya.

Joseph said, "This Adventist couple have become friends to me. My focus is to help children. Theirs was to give water to the people. They have put water access in many places, even here in Kapune. They also helped me to form a constitution for my organization from Isaiah 1:17 to aid children. First, seek justice. Second, plead for orphans. Third, defend the oppressed. And fourth, plead for widows. This is now the constitution I use in helping the children I rescue."

A few months later another American Adventist couple had their imports stolen. They were missionary evangelists coming to install satellite dishes. They told the first couple about it and were told, "Call Joseph!"

This time Joseph called the minster directly, and he acted quickly, sorting everything out in less than an hour.

They asked, "What can we do in thanks, Joseph?"

"First, thank God! Then build a church in my village."

Joseph said later, "They built a church about a thousand feet from my grandfather's house. They also installed a satellite and projector and screen for the church."

Three years later a satellite evangelism program broadcast from South Africa was held at the church. Thirty-seven Maasai were baptized because of the two-week program.

Joseph continued working in Nairobi for another year—until he had earned enough money to come home, buy land, and start his work as a rescuer of children.

Chapter 10

December 29: The Maasai Life

Living here with the Maasai is a very peaceful and enjoyable experience.*
Each morning I wake before dawn and walk out of our mud hut and down the hill to the toilet. When it is dark in Kapune, it is *very* dark. There is no power, so there are no lights other than the stars. A solar panel on the roof provides enough power to charge devices and run two small lights—one in the kitchen and one in the lounge. There has been no moon for the past two nights, so we've had an amazing display of stars!

After walking back up to the house, I get my iPad and spend a couple of hours writing. As the sun rises, so do the roosters. Then the cows begin lowing, and the children wake. The sponsor kids sleep in a room filled with bunk beds just in front of where I sit to write in the lounge. They come out, one by one, into the morning air. Those who remain in the room chat and giggle to themselves. One little boy just came out struggling to zip up his hoodie. He walked over to me for a hug, and then I zipped him up.

The children understand more English than they can speak. While English is the primary language at school, they speak Maasai or Swahili most of the time. Joseph likes to joke that the kids think Swahili and English are the same. They speak a mixed jumble of both.

Maasai children greet an adult by offering the adult the top of their heads. The adult then places a hand gently on the child's head and says, "*Supa*," which means "Hello." On the first day when we arrived, all the

---

* Journal entry for Thursday, December 29, 2016.

Two Maasai women lead the worship procession as they dance and sing worship songs.

children greeted us as we exited the Toyota Prado. After greeting them in their way, I said, "Let me show you how I greet the kids at my schools in Australia." Then I offered them my hand for a high five. Once I got across the language barrier, I got some good high fives and lots of laughter. But later, when I lifted my hand for a high five as I approached any child, they would see my hand and offer the crown of their heads. So today I'm going to try a low five (underhand) and see if I can get some!

Once the *mzungus* begin to wake, preparations for breakfast begin. The small kitchen area is behind the lounge room, which is between the back bedrooms. Cooking is done on a gas stove or on small firepots. The children bring us one of these pots of smoldering charcoal before each meal.

Breakfast for the *mzungus* consists of porridge, cereal, and toast. It is filling and delicious. The children all head down to Joseph and Mercy's house for meals. Due to the very real possibility of getting typhoid from the local water, all food preparation for *mzungus* is done with bottled water brought in from the city. The Maasai stomach is used to the local water. So we prepare food and eat separately.

December 29: The Maasai Life

It is almost 8:00 A.M., and two girls have just come in with makeshift brooms (a handful of palm fronds or a tree branch) and are now sweeping the mud floor. Next, they will bring water and douse the walking area to keep down the dust during the day.

In the two daytime meetings yesterday, Joseph and I told the two Creation stories in Genesis 1 and 2.

Before lunch, as the warm sun shone on the rolling hills, Joseph and I explained how the first Creation story is about God creating good life from chaos. He starts with the mess we are in; and once we say, "I see You, God," He says, "Let there be light," just as He said in the beginning, then there will be light in our lives. And as He continues a good work in us, He leads us to rest in Him. We can go from chaos to meaning, from suffering to Sabbath.

After lunch we watch the Kapune church choir sing and dance in traditional Maasai fashion for nearly an hour. Joseph and I told them the second Creation story. God has a plan and a place for us. From the dusty dirt of loneliness, He creates life—creation, creatures, and community. His plan is that we live in positive relationships: a cord of three is not easily broken. When we love Him first, we will love others not as above us or below us, but as equals. All of us, created in the image of God, are to live in a relationship with Him and with each other.

There were some fantastic questions from two women after we finished. They wanted to know why there are so many abusive husbands if God created woman from the side of man as an equal. So Joseph and I began telling them the great controversy story. My answer, simply, was, "The way you treat other people shows which game you are playing—God's game of putting love first, or Lucifer's game of putting self first."

Today the first meeting will happen sometime midmorning. As Joseph says, "Kenyan time is not like *mzungu* time. We are not so concerned." And it's true! Yesterday's 10:00 A.M. meeting started just before noon. It really doesn't matter, because the people are relaxed and happy and they come for the day.

People walk everywhere, and many of them live miles away, so they walk a lot. Many of the people who come to the meetings walk for more than

Two women sing and dance as they lead in a time of worship.

an hour to get here, and they walk home afterward. It's a peaceful, slow life. It's beautiful.

The Maasai people are 100 percent about community. They do everything together, and they take their time. Just now a group of girls came in to take the chairs that had been stored overnight in the lounge back down to the meeting tent.

Before and after the morning and afternoon meetings yesterday, a choir sang and danced to music they had prerecorded. They danced and sang for hours over the course of the day. Every service was embraced by music. Those who sing and dance do it with joy. And those who watch do so with respect and interest. Joseph said, "The music will be much better tomorrow. Many people could not come because of a funeral."

The writing of this chapter was paused when Joseph came in to tell us more about the Maasai culture. I have just learned about the value of cows, the dowry for a wife, and the system of respect for elders.

Last night fifty-one people packed the small lounge room in our mud house. Most of the day's visitors had begun the long walk home by then,

December 29: The Maasai Life

but some of the children had stayed for the night story. They sang so beautifully, danced with joy, and laughed throughout. Then Joseph and I told them how much Jesus loves them.

After we closed with prayer, many of the children began their long walk home. Joseph explained to them how to be careful on their way home and invited them all back for the next day's meetings.

It's 10:04 a.m. and the morning meeting is due to start soon. Joseph just walked in, and I asked, "Are the people showing up?"

"Yes! They are showing up," Joseph said. "I am expecting them by ten o'clock."

"It's ten oh four," I said.

We laughed together, and Joseph said, "We say there is no hurry in Africa!"

Chapter 11

Maasai Cows

On my first day among the Maasai, Joseph told me a story about a local politician who was trying to win the votes of his fellow Maasai people. He told them he was just like them and held the same values. He said his family meant everything to him. But Joseph said, "We know this is not true because he doesn't have even one cow!"

Joseph explained that the man is rich with money and has a big house. He sends all five of his kids to a private boarding school. "But without cows," Joseph said, "we know he does not really love his family and is not a true Maasai like us."

Joseph sat down with us *mzungus* and explained the importance of the cow to the Maasai. Every cow has a monetary value: a small adult cow costs about twenty thousand shillings (about two hundred US dollars), and a large bull at its prime is worth sixty thousand shillings (about six hundred US dollars). But the monetary value of the cow is a very small part of why Maasai have cows.

A herd of cows shows that the Maasai man who owns them has respect and shows respect to others. At every major event in the life of a Maasai boy, he receives a cow from his father. When his middle two front teeth are removed as a boy, he receives a cow. When he is circumcised at thirteen, he receives a cow. When he becomes a *moran* (a Maasai teen warrior that protects the community), he receives a cow. When he is married, he receives a cow. And when he is considered a real adult, he receives a cow.

"How many cows will you have received by the time you are an adult?" I asked.

"Many cows!" Joseph said.

I asked about the girls. Joseph explained that children and women held value in the same way as the cows in primitive Maasai culture. They show the respectability and wealth of the man. Joseph said, "A man who is married is respected. A man who is married for a long time and has wisdom—like my father who has much wisdom—is respected most of all."

"What about now?" I asked. "Do the Maasai still value women as possessions?"

"Only the primitive Maasai," Joseph said. "The modern Maasai man chooses his own wife and treats her with equal respect. And he loves his children. But we still give the cows!"

When a primitive Maasai man is shown a wife by his parents or a modern Maasai man chooses a wife for himself, he then takes a cow to her father as a gift and says, "I wish to talk to you about marrying your daughter." Then they agree on a dowry. Joseph explained that the dowry is consistent in each clan, and the dowry paid is determined by the clan of the wife-to-be. The dowry does not change based on the perception of the suitor's wealth or the bride's beauty. "Some clans it might be seven cows; some it might be fourteen cows; some more," Joseph stated.

I asked, "Is it rude to ask a Maasai man how many cows he gave for his wife?"

"No," Joseph smiled. "Because it is just about the wife's clan. I gave twenty cows for my wife. And once I am married, I follow the wishes and rules of her clan. I become part of her family."

Once married, the Maasai man gives a cow to his new father-in-law to be allowed to eat under his roof for the rest of his life. If he does not give the cow, he can never eat in his father-in-law's house. This special cow also means that a Maasai man is a full adult. "If a man does not get married," Joseph said, "he cannot be a full adult."

"Never?" I asked.

"If you, David, are not married but wish to shake the hands, you will take a cow to the most respected man in your community. That man, who is very much respected by all the community, will tell everyone that you have given him the cow and are now to be respected as a full adult."

Joseph explained that Maasai men and women are categorized in "age sets." Children are to show respect by offering the crowns of their heads to be touched by anyone in a higher age set. When you leave childhood, the touch moves to your shoulder. When two full adults meet, you shake hands.

"How do you know which age set a person is in when he or she approaches you?" I asked.

"He or she will offer you the correct part of the body," Joseph said.

I have seen this many times during the past few days. Now I understand. Most of the children, when they approach me, make eye contact until they are about a yard away, then they look down and step closer. I had thought they were shy. They were showing me respect and requesting that I receive that respect with a touch.

"What if you touch the wrong part?" I said.

"You give a cow!" Joseph said. "If I touch a married woman's head, I give a cow. If a child touches someone in a higher age set on the head, the child's parents must give a cow. Even if someone else sees it happen from afar, they must report it to the child's father, and a cow must be given."

"Respect is very important to the Maasai," I said.

Joseph said, "So very important! Without respect, the whole community is not strong."

Joseph went on to explain other reasons why a cow is given. Sometimes it is done as a social contract and sometimes as a gift. At weddings, family and close friends bring cows. When a child is born, the family brings a cow for that child. When a child is adopted, the new father gives the child a cow. When a child gets high marks in school, the family will give cows to the father. When a new house is finished, the family will give a cow.

"What if you give the cow to me because my child got good grades and then the next day I gave the same cow back to you for another reason?" I asked.

Joseph laughed. "I have never heard of such a thing happening! But it would not matter. It is your cow when you receive it. You can do what you wish. You can even sell the cow the next day. No offense will be taken."

I asked, "So it's OK to sell the cows if you want money to buy something else?"

"Yes, of course," Joseph said. "But every cow you sell makes you less able to show respect to others. And a small herd means you are not very respected by others."

"A Maasai man wants to keep his cows," I said.

"True!" Joseph said. "The primitive Maasai believed that there was once a beautiful valley, like the Garden of Eden you talked about yesterday, where the Maasai lived. On one edge of the garden, there was a very high cliff. One day all the cows were created on the top of the cliff. The cows jumped down into the valley. This means all cows are given by God to the Maasai."

"All the cows in the world?" I asked.

"Yes," Joseph said. "Every cow in the world is first a Maasai cow."

"That's a great story," I replied. "It shows that the Maasai believe God respects and loves them."

"True!" Joseph said. "But it has a bad side too. If a primitive Maasai man wanted to be a real, brave man, he would steal the cows from tribes who were not Maasai."

"Because the cows were God's gift to the Maasai," I said.

"Yes," Joseph said. "But this is not the way of the modern Maasai. Stealing is against the law and brings disrespect."

After a thoughtful pause, Joseph continued, "There are many other reasons why a Maasai gives a cow. If a Maasai does something to anger another Maasai, he can give a cow to cool the other person's anger, so he or she will respond kindly. A respected family member, not involved in the conflict, can also bring a cow to ask the offended person as a plea.

"For example, if a wife has an affair, the wife's father gives the husband a cow, then says, 'Please consider carefully. You are both my children.' This usually helps. The decision still belongs to the offended party, but the cow softens the heart and invites careful reflection. It also shows the respect of the family member who gave the cow.

"If you injure someone, a certain number of cows is required. Every part of the body has a price in cows. If you draw blood from any other Maasai in anger," Joseph said, "you must give one cow."

I asked, "What's the worst thing? What requires the most cows?"

Joseph stated, "Murder. If you kill another Maasai, you must give forty-nine cows."

"That could take all your cows!" I said.

"Yes," Joseph replied. "But a Maasai must respect other Maasai."

"It certainly explains why you are such gentle people!" I said. "A few generations of living like this, and you would learn to be gentle and show respect to everyone."

Joseph said, "True. There is one more time a Maasai man gives a cow. It is a very special ritual. It is when one man chooses his *olkiteng loolbaa*—a very special friend. This friend is your equal. You tell him everything, and he tells you everything. If this man tells you to do anything, you must do it.

"My *olkiteng loolbaa* helps me do the right thing. He will challenge me when I do the wrong thing. I must do what he says. If I do something wrong, he will go to the panel of elders to seek wisdom. Then he will bring their wisdom to me. And I do the same for him. A Maasai can never be a leader in the community without having an *olkiteng loolbaa*."

Joseph then explained the process of choosing a lifelong *olkiteng loolbaa*. "Once a Maasai man chooses his special friend, he must sit with the man's family and tell them he has chosen their son to be his *olkiteng loolbaa*. The family must agree before you choose this man. They will tell you if he is a man of respect worthy of being your *olkiteng loolbaa*.

"Then you have a special ceremony." Joseph continued, "In the ceremony, you bring a perfect, full-grown bull—no blemishes on its coat or anything wrong with the bull, such as a bad eye or something. This bull is slaughtered, and a party is given for everyone from the age set and both families. After the celebration, the men give each other a cow."

This choosing of the *olkiteng loolbaa* is central to the culture of respect for the Maasai. The men are both mentors and accountability partners that seek and give wisdom to each other for the rest of their lives. It is an agreement of goodwill, ensuring that the community will be strong.

In the Maasai culture, the cow is everything. It is the glue that holds the community together. It is the currency used to maintain relationships and show respect. When a child or anyone in an age set lower than a full adult dies, he or she is buried next to the house. When a full adult dies, he or she is buried in the cow pen. "It is a sign of the greatest respect." Joseph said, "We will not even move the pen to another place for more than one month."

A Maasai man who has all the money in the world but has no cows is not a real Maasai. Joseph explained, "A house is not a home until it has a wife and a cow." The lack of cows near this politician's house demonstrates that he has been shown no respect by others. His lack of cows also means he can show no respect to his children or anyone else in the community. And when he dies, he will be buried in shame.

Chapter 12

December 30: Expect Anything in Kenya

Within my first few minutes in Kenya, as we were driving away from the airport, Carole said, "There is a clear plan laid out for the next three weeks, but anything can happen in Kenya. So expect anything!"*

Yesterday, as the morning meeting ended, wailing could be heard down the valley. A few of the Maasai young men took off running to see what it was.

I walked up alongside Joseph and asked, "What has happened?"

"Something bad," he said. "The wailing means something has happened."

"What kind of wail is it?" I asked.

He said, "Someone is very injured or very sick. Maybe worse."

There are three kinds of Maasai wailing. Each is intended to convey a different story to neighbors. There is a wail for injury, a wail for death, and a wail for stolen cows.

Joseph pulled out his mobile phone and called a number. He talked in Maasai for less than a minute and then hung up.

He said, "A four-year-old girl has just died in a house down there. We knew she was not well yesterday. But it was worse than that."

"What happens now?" I asked.

"There will be a funeral," Joseph replied. "But not a big one or a long one because it is a small child. It will go for one or maybe two hours."

"Why is it less than other funerals?" I asked.

---

* Journal entry for Friday, December 30, 2016.

December 30: Expect Anything in Kenya

"A funeral is when people come to show respect and tell stories of the person who died." Joseph said, "A small child has few stories and has received only a little respect. People will come to give respect to her parents and family, but there will be few stories for a life so short."

Late that night the message came through the Maasai "grapevine" that the funeral would be the next day. Joseph said, "Very quick, because it is not needed to give time for people to come. To show our respect, we will not have a meeting while the funeral is happening."

This morning Joseph came to our house and said it was up to us if we wanted to go to the funeral. He gave reasons both for going and against going: "You will show respect by showing up, but you will also present them with a dilemma of what to do with you. We give much respect to *mzungus*. They may not want to weep in front of you. There will be much need to weep for a little child dying."

After deciding that we would stay here and work on various projects, Joseph said, "Also, could you all come have a look at Vivian? Her ankle is not better today." We had been told the night before that a child had pulled a muscle.

"Can she stand on it?" Courtney asked.

"No," Joseph said, "not at all."

Carole said, "That's not good. Can she move her toes?"

"No," Joseph replied. "I don't think so."

"It could be broken, Joseph. We might need to take her to a hospital. We will come look now," Carole said.

We walked down to Joseph's house. He picked up seven-year-old Vivian and brought her out into the sunlight. There was not a tear in her eyes, and she didn't make a noise. Her ankle was swollen but not as much as a sprain should be.

I reached down to the good foot and said, "Can you wiggle these toes, like this?" Joseph translated. I closed and opened my hand. She wiggled her toes on the good foot.

"Now this foot," I said, opening and closing my fingers near the other foot. "Can you wiggle these?"

She tried and grimaced in pain. One toe moved slightly.

Carole said, "We need to get her to a hospital. We will go get the Prado."

Normally, a motorcycle taxi is called, and the injured person rides on the back to the hospital. It is a blessing that Leon and Carole were present with a vehicle. Just a few weeks ago, a pregnant neighbor woman had been in labor for four days in her house before a neighbor called Joseph for help. She was taken to hospital on the back of a motorcycle taxi! Unfortunately, both she and the child died in the hospital.

"This is why I have enrolled to learn to drive," Joseph told Courtney. "We must have a vehicle for these children for emergencies. And I must learn to drive!"

The trip to the hospital would be a long, bumpy journey back down the worst road in Kenya. Courtney offered to drive. Two other Maasai girls rode in the back with Vivian.

As she walked out the door of our Maasai mud house, Courtney said, "You'll definitely be writing the story of this day!"

"I've already started," I said, looking up from my writing table.

"The end of the story is yet to happen," Carole said as she followed Courtney.

"I'm sure your day will be filled with adventure," I replied. "It will be a chapter all its own, no doubt."

Once the group were off on their journey, Joseph and I sat down for a marathon storytelling and writing session.

I told Joseph, "You know, Carole told us anything can happen in Kenya."

"True," he said, "very true!"

Chapter 13

December 31: Opening Sabbath

Sabbath began with a sense of frustration and need.*

On Friday, Courtney and Carole had driven all the way to St. Joseph's Mission Hospital in Kilgoris and waited for more than three hours in a typical Kenyan queue—only to be told there was no X-ray machine at this hospital and they would need to go to a different one tomorrow because closing time had passed. Little Vivian was untreated; her ankle was still immobile and in pain.

While they had waited in the hospital, the skies opened and the stony, rut-strewn road became a mudslide. Driving home, Courtney did her best not to careen off the road and managed to get just a few miles from home when she noticed something wasn't right with the vehicle's handling. The group stopped and explored the problem. One of the rear tires was flat.

After a bit of phone tag with Leon and me, we exchanged pictures, and Leon decided it was too flat to drive on. He called a motorcycle taxi and waited. When the taxi arrived more than thirty minutes later, Leon chased it to the top of the hill as it wasn't powerful enough to take two people up a steep hill. At the top of the hill, Leon hopped on, arrived at the Prado, and fixed the tire quickly.

Soon (Kenyan time) everyone was home. Vivian was back, resting in her bed, and Courtney and Carole were happy to be back. The time, now about 7:30 p.m., was nearing for opening Sabbath.

---

* Journal entry for Saturday morning, December 31, 2016.

A quick meal of potato and pumpkin mash and beans on toast was quickly eaten before the children filled the room for opening Sabbath worship. The topic was prayer, as the day had been filled with prayer. We sang, laughed, prayed, and worshiped together.

Afterward, all the children headed to their beds and so did the adults. It had been a tiring day.

On Sabbath morning, I arose at about 6:00 A.M., and after a trip down the hill to the toilet and back up the hill to my room, I grabbed my towel and toiletries and headed back down the hill. As I went down, I saw the fire where water is heated for a Maasai shower. I went to the fire with my towel over my shoulder and leaned against a tree to enjoy the flames.

Soon Mercy came over with a large pot of water and put it on the flames. I was amazed to watch as she moved the burning logs with her bare hands. I greeted her, and she offered me a chair—the Maasai are wonderfully polite people. I said the ground was closer to the fire.

She said, "Yes, but maybe it is wet."

I smiled and gestured at the fire. "Joseph told me that when the Maasai get wet they build a fire."

Mercy laughed and said, "True!"

Later Joseph came over, and I asked him about touching the burning fire. "Doesn't it hurt?"

He laughed and said, "No, these black hands do not absorb so much heat." Then he took the pot off some crackling logs, reached into the fire, and started moving things around. I was in pain just watching. Finally, he said, "Now that is better for the pot." He replaced the pot on the more balanced arrangement of fuel and showed me his hands. They were fine.

Mercy returned to join us at the fire and tested the water, pouring some into her palm. "Your shower is ready," she said. She then picked the pot up by the rim, poured the water into a large plastic bowl, and carried it to the other room next to the toilet.

A Maasai shower is the fine art of throwing water at yourself from a bowl, soaping up, and then throwing more water at yourself to rinse. Washing your hair is done last above the bowl, so there is some water remaining. You rinse into the bowl, and the water in the bowl gets soapier as your hair

December 31: Opening Sabbath

gets rinsed clean. That's the theory, anyway.

As I reached into the bowl of water, I found it so hot I could barely touch it. I dipped my hands in quickly and rubbed them together. Doing this a few times, I was soon able to handle the heat. Then I began the throwing, soaping, and rinsing process. It is remarkably pleasurable.

After returning to the house, dressing in my Sabbath finest, and having a breakfast of porridge, I saw Joseph and Mercy coming for a visit. They had gifts. "Please accept these poor gifts as our thanks," Joseph said. He then proceeded to hand out the most amazingly beautiful Maasai clothing to us.

Leon and I received handmade shirts. Courtney received a young woman's outfit of a skirt, top, and shawl. Carole was given an adult woman's dress. All the items were truly remarkable in craftsmanship and design.

They waited for us to put them on. Leon and Carole's gifts were a perfect fit. Courtney's had some extra room in it.

Joseph said, "You must eat more *ugali* [cornmeal porridge]. There is room for you to become a woman!"

Courtney laughed.

We are all noticing minor differences in cultural niceties. In Maasai land, one's body shape and size are just topics for discussion like the rain and the cows.

My shirt was too snug to get over my girth.

Joseph said, "Let me help."

I put the beautiful shirt over my shoulders, and he began to tug at the waistline of the shirt.

"No problem," he said, "we will have the maker of the shirt add some."

I removed the shirt from my head and returned to my room to grab one of my collection of pullover Indian-style shirts that my mother-in-law makes for me. They are my favorite shirts! Noticing that the cut and design of the Maasai shirt was very similar, I gave a shirt to Joseph and said, "They can use this as a sizing pattern. It fits perfectly."

"That will help, I am sure," Joseph said.

We put the two shirts in a bag that Carole and Leon took into Kilgoris when heading to the hospital. Joseph called the tailor, and the bag was retrieved from Carole at the hospital.

I said, "I am very sorry. I feel bad for not receiving your gift well."

"Do not worry," Joseph replied. "I guessed all of your sizes, and I am sorry I got yours wrong. You are bigger than you look!"

I laughed, "Yes, I put on weight very evenly everywhere, so I do not have just a big belly or a big bum; it is all big together! Most people are surprised when they hear the number of pounds I weigh."

The road below Joseph's property that leads to the creek and then up to the Kapune Adventist Church.

Joseph looked around. We were alone, so he leaned in and whispered, "What is that number?"

I laughed. Our cultures are so different. But it is amazingly disarming when you realize the Maasai are not being rude, but are truly honest, open, and interested in you. "Two hundred and seventy-five pounds," I said.

His eyes shot wide open.

"Two months ago, the number was two hundred and ninety-seven!" I added. "I am getting smaller, but it takes time."

"True," Joseph said. "I will make the shirt to fit you now. You come stay in Maasai land for three months, and you will be much smaller!"

I said, "True! There is so much walking and natural food. This is a very healthy place."

"Very healthy," Joseph repeated in agreement.

A few minutes later Leon and Carole headed back to Kilgoris with two girls to the district hospital. Vivian could only put a bit of pressure on her foot and wiggle her toes a little. The second girl, Michelle, had developed an infection on her ankle overnight. It was so bad she could hardly walk.

December 31: Opening Sabbath

The four of them got in the Prado and headed to Kilgoris.

Courtney and I joined Joseph and Mercy for the twenty-minute walk to church. Down through the bottom gate we walked, then on to a road that was more of a walking track and past a few houses. Joseph told us who lived in each. We entered a valley with a stream in the middle and crossed a small bridge made from a concrete pipe. Then we walked up a hill toward the church and crossed the field to a group of people clustered under a tree, studying the Bible together. As we walked, we went around the children, sitting on a grassy slope having their Sabbath School class.

We were seated in a position of honor in the front and joined the conversation. Visitors are given respect in Maasai culture, and *mzungus* are clearly visitors. Before you even introduce yourself, it is known that you are a visitor, and you will be shown respect. Courtney and I were given comfortable chairs with backs on them while everyone else sat on the ground or benches.

The lesson was about Job. Speaking about Job's return to health and wealth—having many goats and cows—the pastor taught as the local livestock created the backdrop behind him. The sun shone, and a gentle breeze blew through the trees.

I turned to Courtney and said, "I could do Sabbath like this every week."

She nodded and whispered, "I was just thinking the same thing."

After Sabbath School, there was a lengthy time of singing. One person would start singing where he or she was sitting. Then the person would stand, walk to the front, and gesture to the people he or she wanted to join in. Soon a makeshift choir was formed, and the entire assembly would join in the singing. Then they would sit, and another song would start in the same way.

After a few songs, Joseph invited Courtney and me to go into the church building to plan the service. A church-worship plan book was handed to him, and we divided up the responsibilities. Courtney would do the opening prayer. Joseph and the pastor would do the welcome and pastoral prayer. I would do the sermon (yes, I knew this ahead of time). We then returned to the outdoor church setting and sat behind the table, facing the audience, ready for the service.

The service started with a local choir who performed a beautiful item. The service proceeded as planned and concluded after Joseph and I finished our sermon on "A Day in the Life of Jesus," taught from Matthew 14. It was a joyful and beautiful experience worshiping God with such lovely people in such an amazing setting!

Chapter 14

Vivian's Story

When you see Vivian's deeply trusting eyes, her happy face, and gentle personality, it is hard to believe she has come from a truly terrible place. Just yesterday, while listening to the choir sing and dance, little Vivian sat next to me. Her bandaged food rested on a chair in front of her, and her head rested on my arm, which was draped across the back of her chair. She was completely at peace trusting me, a *mzungu* man she had met earlier in the week.

When Vivian was two years old, she watched from the corner of a room as her father beat her mother into unconsciousness. How many times Vivian saw her father do this is unknown, but one thing is certain—she remembers watching. Joseph said, "Sometimes she is crying because she remembers."

When Vivian's mother didn't wake up, she was taken to the hospital where she died. Because Vivian's mother had been from a different tribe than her father, no one around Vivian wanted to care for her once her mother was gone.

Not wanting to accept the murder for what it was, the man's family did not have a burial service for Vivian's mother. "They buried her like a dog," Joseph said. "Just placed her in a hole with no service."

When word got back to Vivian's grandmother that her daughter was dead, she came to claim Vivian and her three-month-old sister. When she arrived, the parents of Vivian's father tried to give her a cow to replace her daughter. She rejected the cow, saying, "A cow is not worth enough for my daughter." She then asked if she could have the two children.

Even though they did not want the children, they refused to give them to the grandmother because they knew Vivian could remember what she saw. They did not want the story to get out. So they kept her, hoping she would forget.

Vivian's grandmother went home without her granddaughters and without any sense of closure about her daughter's death. She figured out that her daughter had been murdered because of the stories she heard and the way she was treated by the husband's family.

The girls went to their other grandmother instead. This grandmother had no compassion on the children and treated them poorly. Within the year, she decided to make some money by selling Vivian to a barren woman. A dowry was paid for Vivian, and she moved into the home of the barren woman. Vivian was being trained to be a surrogate womb for this woman.

In primitive Maasai culture, a barren woman can take a girl to be her wife. The woman raises her and trains her to be a good wife, to bear children for her, and to continue her lineage. Some girls are taken very young. These girls are called the barren women's wives because they physically replace the barren women over time.

In the years of prepubescent training, the girl will often sleep alongside a man of her "wife's" choosing—not for sexual purposes, but to help the girl become a woman faster. Primitive Maasai believe that a girl will grow her breasts and hips faster if she is sleeping next to a man. This makes her ready to have children as soon as possible.

Barren women marrying young girls as wives is still very common today, even among modern Maasai. It is perceived as the only way out of barrenness.

"This is child slavery," Joseph said. "This child, as soon as she is old enough to bear children, will be sold for the night to whomever her wife demands. She has no rights.

"Vivian had been told by her wife, 'We are the only people protecting you. Everyone else will murder you like your mother.' The brainwashing, in four years with no school and all these lies, leads to the girl believing this is the life for her."

The elder of the local Seventh-day Adventist church was a woman who knew Vivian's wife and was trusted by her. She came in and out of her

Vivian's Story

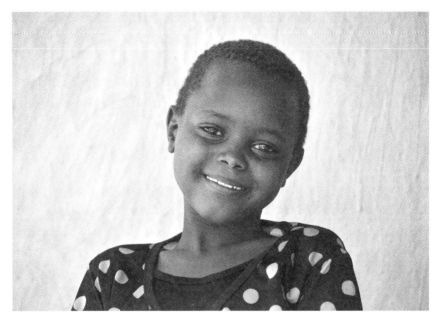

Vivian watched as her mother was beaten to death.
She was being groomed by a married woman to be
a forced second wife when Joseph rescued her.

house as a trusted friend. The elder, too, was a friend of Joseph. She called him and told him Vivian's story. She said, "If we do not rescue this girl very soon, she will be brainwashed for life."

Joseph called Carole and asked if Education Care Projects—Kenya had received funds recently and could support one more. He told Carole the whole story and due to the kindness of some Australian partners, Vivian's safety, clothing, schooling, and basic needs were assured.

"When I first started," Joseph said, "I wanted to save just one life. Each time I do, I start again. Vivian is the one life this time."

Financial assistance assured, Joseph called the elder and told her he would come rescue Vivian. The elder went in for a visit while the barren woman was doing chores and told Vivian, "God is sending a special man to save you. He will take you to a safe place."

"Vivian was already believing the brainwashing," Joseph said. "The years of hatred from her father and grandmother and now the fear of death instilled in her by her wife—she was not willing to be rescued."

The elder continued visiting Vivian until she saw hope in her eyes. She called Joseph and said, "She is ready to be rescued."

Joseph stated, "It was a very small one-room house and very poorly built. I rescued her at night. The barren woman was sleeping in the house of the man who was helping to train Vivian. The elder and I quietly went into the house to rescue Vivian from where she was sleeping alone.

"I took her straight to the school. It was her first time to wear shoes and first time to sleep on a mattress.

"I reported the rescue to the government. While they appreciate what I am doing, they fear the cultural consequences. It is a difficult situation."

As he was telling us Vivian's story, Joseph mentioned to Carole another barren widow who also has a young girl as a wife. Carole was amazed. "But she is a lovely lady!" Carole exclaimed. "How can she do something so horrible?"

"She is destitute," Joseph said. "No one will care for widows, and she believes she must care for herself in this way."

Carole replied, "But she is an Adventist. She needs to find a better way!"

"Yes," Joseph said, "I am telling her this. I am telling her to treat her wife as just a daughter. Raise her as her own child. The child she has is an orphan and needs a mother. I am asking her, 'Do not teach her as a wife. Please, sister, do not teach her these things.' She is saying she will do this."

"Will she?" Carole asked.

"She will," Joseph said. "She is. She is telling me she is only raising her like a daughter now."

Carole said, "Oh, Joseph, we really need to do more for the widows."

"We are trying," Joseph replied. "We give them work to do and pay them. We provide some food. We are rescuing the widows too."

Chapter 15

December 31: Closing Sabbath

After the service was finished, we had Communion, as this was Thirteenth Sabbath.* First, we had the footwashing, with the men outside and the women in the church. Joseph and I washed each other's feet and prayed together. Then he washed my hands and offered his to me to wash. It is customary to wash your hands after footwashing to prepare for taking the bread and wine, but I had never had someone else wash them. It was a remarkably humbling and touching moment. As we finished the handwashing, Joseph took my hands in his and prayed for me.

Then we went into the church for the bread and wine. Courtney and I were unsure if we should drink the "wine" because it could be watered down with river water, which the people drink, and we could get sick. After being assured the juice was received from the conference and then boiled, Mercy said to Courtney, "But you need not worry, it has been prayed for. You will not get sick." She was right; we are both fine and healthy a day later.

Communion finished at two-thirty. Leon had arrived at the end of the service and gave his greetings to the people. He told them how much he and Carole had enjoyed their time with them and how much they would miss them when they left on Wednesday.

As we exited the church and stood around outside, a few ladies started looking over at the Prado, parked just beyond the fence and laughing. A

---

* Journal entry for Saturday evening, December 31, 2016.

wet weather jacket was hanging from the window, as the window had not been closing properly.

I said to Joseph, "Are they laughing about the coat in the window?"

"No," Joseph said, "they are talking about you."

"Me?" I asked. "Why?"

"They are wondering if you will fit through the hole in the fence to get to the Prado," Joseph laughed.

The fence had a gate that you ducked through rather than opened. It consisted of several sticks crossed and nailed together. There was a hole, clearly big enough for a Maasai to go through but not a goat or cow.

I laughed and headed toward the fence. "I'll show them!" I said over my shoulder.

I ducked and squeezed through the hole as casually as I could. Then, popping up on the other side, I spun around and blew a raspberry.

They all laughed.

Heading back up the hill in the Prado, Leon gave us an update. Michelle had a badly infected ankle. It was treated and wrapped, and she was given medicine to take regularly to get rid of the infection.

The X-ray showed that little Vivian had a chipped bone in her ankle. Her leg was wrapped, and she was under strict orders not to walk on it. She got around with a stick and a smile. She would stay home for the next week and then join the children heading to school on Wednesday after their two-month, year-end holiday.

The ridge above Joseph's property in Kapune, Kenya.

After a lunch of spaghetti

December 31: Closing Sabbath

on toast, we headed up to the ridge for a walk, surrounded by the most amazing views. All the children walked with us, and we were joined by more kids as we walked out of the village.

Along the ridge, I was intrigued by an empty metal frame. Clearly it had once had a sign in it. I asked Joseph about it.

"People from the Netherlands planted trees and put up the sign," Joseph said.

I looked across the barren mountaintop. "What trees?" I asked.

Joseph pointed at one lone tree some way up the ridge. "That is the last one." Then he pointed at rocky circles in the ground. "These are holes where the trees were."

Perceiving them for the first time, I saw a huge gridwork of holes in all directions. "What happened to the rest of the trees?"

"They planted them and left," Joseph answered. "The government said they would care for them, but they did nothing."

I said, "The people from the Netherlands went home thinking they had done a great thing. I wonder what they would think now."

"True," Joseph said.

"Why did they plant the trees here?" I asked.

"The government owns the tops of all the highest ridges," Joseph said. "They allow good things like schools and clinics there. But the government does not run them."

We continued walking up the ridge.

Leon led songs as he walked with a group far in front of us. I made animal noises at the occasional donkey, cow, and sheep. The kids laughed and joined in.

At the top of the ridge, we were blessed with a beautiful, lengthy sunset. The children ran and played as the *mzungus* took photos of themselves, the kids, the views, and everything else.

As we walked, the children held our hands. Some got rides on the shoulders of Joseph and myself. It was a perfect finish to a blessed Sabbath day.

The day that had started with frustration and angst at the slowness of this place ended with gratitude for the pace. The peace and tranquility were revitalizing. Knowing that the two girls who were injured were now on the mend allowed everyone to rest their worried minds and enjoy the ebbing minutes of the Sabbath.

We returned to the house and had a quick dinner of pan-fried potatoes—Leon's specialty. Then we held a time of singing and stories about the great plan God has for our eternal life and the intricate design He has for each of our lives here on Earth, should we choose to follow Him.

We closed the Sabbath, as we had opened it, with prayer. Then we all went to bed.

Chapter 16

January 3: Walk-Ins

On our final day in Kapune, we had a number of walk-ins.* Stories of *mzungus* teaching about Jesus and helping children were reaching areas further than our daily visitors walked.

At midmorning four children walked in. Joseph explained that the oldest girl, Purity, was expected. Her grandmother had called the night before, telling him about Purity and asking if she could meet the *mzungus*. Once it was clear she was coming, Purity invited three street children to join her. Their mother is mentally handicapped, spending her days eating food scraps off the road where people throw them and occasionally becoming pregnant due to men who take advantage of her simple mind to get to her body.

As we sat with the four children, who had walked twelve and a half miles to reach us, Joseph interpreted their stories. Purity is thirteen years old and lives with her grandmother. Her parents are both dead. She loves school and wants to go to high school this year, but her grandmother cannot afford it.

"If no one takes her," Joseph said, "she will be married." The grandmother considers her job finished; Purity is ready to move on to marriage or education.

The other three children—Angela, thirteen; Faith, ten; and Amos, six—are looking for an education as well. Family members are caring for them

---

* Journal entry for Tuesday, January 3, 2017.

as their mother is unable to do it. Angela will likely be married off to provide for her mother and siblings. When Faith reaches the age of thirteen, the same thing faces her. All three of them are only receiving an education when the problems of life allow them to attend the local government school where the education is very poor.

As the children went outside for photos to be used to find sponsors, Joseph poured his heart out to me. "How do I know who God wants me to take?" he asked. "These three with the sick mother are just like baby birds fallen out of a nest. They need help to live."

Purity and three street children who came to visit the *muzungus*, hoping for sponsors to make their education possible.

Joseph paused. "I am taking phone calls and walk-ins like this so many times—maybe three times a week—and I add them to my book, then an emergency comes where I must act." Joseph, clearly overwhelmed by the scale of need in his community, continued, "I ask God to give me direction, so I know what to do."

As the first meeting finished and we broke for lunch, Joseph approached me. "A handicapped woman has walked all day to get here. She wants prayer."

Carole, Courtney, Joseph, and I gathered in the lounge room and received the woman and her friend.

Rose lost the lower half of her left leg to a horrible infection in a wound caused by a thorn. After the leg went black, she went to receive help. When people live so far from town and even further from medical attention, small injuries often become life-threatening illnesses. She was told she would die if the dead part of her leg was not removed. The leg was amputated last March. Her prayer request was for strength and courage.

Rose lives with her husband, a schoolteacher in their village, and five children between the ages of two and eighteen. She is very proud of them but is frustrated that she cannot care for them as she used to. We each took turns praying for Rose and then gave her words of comfort—telling our own stories—and encouragement. Then hugs and handshakes were exchanged, and Rose stood with the aid of her crutches and left.

Later that afternoon four more children arrived. Four-year-old Brian is the child of a teenage rape victim. He has lived with a kind lady with a large but poor family in his village. His mother ran away in shame the day he was born. He is ready for school but has no family to fund it.

Twelve-year-old Miriam is being looked after by her aunt because her mother also ran away in shame after her birth. She is in school and doing well, but she would love to go to a boarding school where the education and care are much better at than government schools.

The mother of fourteen-year-old Charlene died while giving birth to her, and her father ran away because he had no wife. Charlene lived with her grandmother until she was two years old and was then given to her older brother. Even though he is much older than she is, he has a house but no wife. Charlene has been taking care of all the wifely duties in the home of her brother since she went to live with him. Charlene would love to go to boarding school.

Thirteen-year-old Lekini was asleep in bed next to his brother when seven men broke the door down and hacked his brother to death. They left Lekini with three huge knife cuts on his head and a gash on the top of his forearm, from wrist to elbow. Thinking both boys were dead, the men went outside the house and sang a victory song before disappearing into the night.

Joseph was called, and he held the dying boy on his lap for the next ten hours as they tried to find an open hospital that could help with such severe wounds. "Most of the skin on top of his head was hanging off the side," Joseph said. "This boy is a miracle. He bled so much, but he is alive because of God."

As Lekini sat before us, he told us he wants to be a lawyer one day. The police have told Joseph they have the names of all seven men. "But who will be a witness?" they asked him. The stories have been told, but the crime was not witnessed. Only with a witness can these men be tried. No wonder Lekini wants to be a lawyer.

As Lekini walked out of our mud hut, our hearts were heavy. There was so much need revealed in just one day.

Carole asked me a few times over the evening, "What will your blog be about tomorrow morning?"

"The walk-ins we had today," I replied.

During the night, Carole couldn't sleep. She was so deeply affected by Lekini's story that she wrote it and placed it on Facebook.

Lekini, who has been living with his uncle since the attack, was invited to come back to Joseph's house. We had something wonderful to tell him. By the time the sun rose here in Kenya, an Australian friend of Carole and Leon read the post and was moved to help. Lekini would be going to school.

Today was the first day of school. The children in Joseph's program who had been on vacation for the past two months were heading back to their safe schools for an education.

Purity stayed the night, intending to walk home today. Instead, due to some more amazing partners found overnight, Carole and Joseph told her this morning that she would be walking to school with the children.

"She was beaming!" Carole said.

"Yes, she was most excited!" Joseph added.

Today two children—Lekini and Purity—did not return to their lives of trauma, but were sent to receive an education. "They need hope," Carole said. "Education gives them hope for the future because they can choose a better life."

Angela, Faith, Amos, Brian, Miriam, and Charlene have returned home where they will hope and pray that one day they, too, will be able to attend a safe school and receive an education that will give them hope and a future.

Chapter 17

David's Story

"My first hope was to save just one life," Joseph said. "But once I had saved David, it became my passion to do it again and again. This is my life."

David was also the first child to be taken into the Education Care Projects—Kenya program. While these two beginnings were a few years apart, David's story has deep roots for both Joseph and Carole. His life inspired them to save many more.

When David's mother got married, she was already pregnant with another man's child. Her husband decided that he would have the baby killed after it was born. While this is illegal, it still happens in many places in Africa.

At just three weeks old, David was laid on the ground at the gate of a cattle pen. When the cattle were driven out of the pen in a rush, it was expected that the tiny infant would be crushed. This method is used to shame the mother as the clan comes to watch as a child of adultery is killed. The witnesses are expected to say, "Because of your adultery, you have caused this painful death!"

Joseph said, "David's mother stood at the edge of the gate and watched as the cows were pushed toward her child lying at the gate. She fainted from the shock of what was about to occur. But a miracle happened! All the cows rushed over him without one stepping on him. There wasn't even a mark on his blanket."

After the cows passed and David was not smashed, the Maasai told David's mother to take her child. Many witnesses told Joseph the story. They saw David live through the impossible.

Knowing the hatred of David's stepfather, his mother knew that attempts would continue to be made on his life. She took the child to her mother and gave David to her. But David's grandfather said to his wife, "If I let this child grow up in my house, the community will say we approve of prostitution and adultery. Maybe those cows don't know how to trample properly. My cows are better."

Realizing the threat was real, the grandmother fled with David to her son's house—the home of David's uncle. Unmarried but living a long way away, the uncle was the safest option she could find.

David was the first child rescued by Joseph and the first child taken into the Education Care Projects—Kenya program.

David stayed with his uncle until he was two years old. Then David's uncle got married. His uncle's wife did not want David and mistreated him. She did not want to look after a child whose parents had rejected him. She starved and hurt David. The uncle did not like this and beat his wife. This made her hate David even more.

One day, while the uncle was selling cows at a market, his wife took David to the middle of a forest, tied his hands and feet to a tree, gagged him, and left him there. David stayed like that for four days.

When his uncle came home, his wife would not tell him what she had done with David. His uncle asked the community to start wailing a death wail. This causes the Maasai warriors called *morans* to come running to see what is to be done. Morans are the unmarried Maasai men. They are the fittest and fastest runners. After the *morans* hear the reason for the wailing, they return to their homes and take the message back to their communities.

David's uncle asked everyone to help search for David. The communities ran to the forests and searched for three days. On the fourth day, hunters from Tanzania heard their dogs barking. They hadn't heard about the search for David and thought the dogs had cornered a wild animal. The hunters tried to ignore the dogs, but the dogs would not stop barking. When the hunters followed their dogs, they were led to the tree where David was tied.

David was unconscious, and the hunters thought he might be dead. They untied him, ungagged him, and took him to a nearby village. Because of the wailing a few days before, the people in this small community knew where the child was from.

David was taken to a mission hospital, where he was treated well. David recovered but developed a condition in which he would lose consciousness and shake.

While David was in the hospital, the story reached Joseph, and he rescued the boy. Long before the time of Education Care Projects—Kenya, Joseph sought help from a local politician who agreed to pay for the hospital bills and provide funds for David's schooling and other needs.

When David reached the age of circumcision (thirteen years old), David's original family was upset that he was supported by the local politician and told him to stop because he was hurting their culture.

It was at this time that Joseph met Carole and Leon and asked them for help. In 2013, David was the first student to become part of Education Care Projects—Kenya.

Today, a young adult at nineteen years old, David is passionate about the animals of Kenya and wants to become a tour guide. He is a very practical man and a good organizer.

"What I love about David," Joseph said, "is that when he sees someone else being treated unfairly, he will not keep quiet. He is always ready to stand up for others."

While the two events were years apart, David was the shared starting point for Joseph's rescue work and the partnership with Education Care

Projects—Kenya. Joseph said, "When you see all this project does, you cannot deny that God is doing everything. Without the Holy Spirit helping us every day, we could not do what we do."

Chapter 18

January 4:
Leaving Kapune

Our first and last mornings in Maasai land had the same story.*
During both nights, a neighbor's cows had been stolen. The wailing began, and Maasai men from all around came running.

This time they caught up with the cows, and the thieves ran away in fear. The cows were taken back to the rightful owner, and the men all returned home.

"But first we must sing a song," Joseph said.

"A song?" I asked.

"Yes," Joseph replied, "there is a special song we sing only when the cows are rescued safely."

He looked at me with a sly smile, knowing what he was about to say would make me laugh. "And we kill one cow and roast it up for a celebration."

"You kill one of the cows you just rescued?" I asked, raising my eyebrows.

"Yes!" Joseph laughed. "It is required."

"Then you come home to sleep?" I asked.

"A little bit," Joseph said.

Carole asked, "Do your cows ever get stolen?"

Joseph looked at her like she had asked a ridiculous question.

"No, of course not!"

"Because your pen is so close to your house?" Carole asked.

---

* Journal entry for Wednesday, January 4, 2017.

The revival tent used for the daily meetings. The people who walked from distant places spill out of the sides of the tent.

Joseph said, "No. Because I have God."

* * * * *

This morning was filled with packing and pictures. The kids were packing to head off to school. We were packing to head out on the next leg of our journey for Hands of Hope Academy near Eldoret.

The packing and planning were interrupted many times for pictures, farewells, hugs, and handshakes.

My resized Maasai shirt arrived this morning, and Joseph presented it to me. It was a perfect fit!

When Courtney wore her Maasai clothes to church, she was given a Maasai name—Nashipai. It means "someone who is filled with compassion on the inside and joy on the outside—always caring and always happy."

Our time here in Maasai land has left a permanent mark on our hearts. Last night during the farewell speeches from the leaders of the Kapune Seventh-day Adventist Church, the deep darkness of a Kenyan night had

January 4: Leaving Kapune

fallen, but the hearts in the meeting tent in Joseph's yard were filled with the light of God.

Such kind things were said by each person, thanking us for our ministry to them during this week and for the ongoing ministry of Carole and Leon to the Maasai community in Kapune. At some point in each person's speech, we were begged, "Please do not forget Kapune!" When Joseph asked me to say a few words, I told them, "In our country, we say, 'Home is where the heart is.' Because this is true, we will never leave you. Thank you for loving us."

Our hearts will always be with the beautiful and deeply passionate people in Kapune. Their story is now our story, and we will not forget them.

Chapter 19

January 5: First-World Problems

In life, there are special days that open the world to you through the difficulties you experience.* Yesterday was one of those days.

Leaving Joseph's property, we drove to the school that Education Care Projects—Kenya is building to provide safety and education to the children rescued in Maasai land. We stopped and snapped a few photos of the school's foundation and the beginning of the walls. Leon would return later to continue the building project.

Once finished at the school, we drove back down the worst road in Kenya to get to the nearest village, where we purchased a lunch of *chapatis*—a local flatbread that is a cross between a tortilla and a crêpe, served very hot. They are very delicious!

We went back up the road toward Joseph's house but turned left before reaching it. We wove our way along a dirt track that took us through many small villages. Using Google maps and Leon's local knowledge, we navigated our way to a tarmac road more than two hours' drive from the beginning of our day's journey.

When we reached Kisii, the first large town, we stopped to have two punctured tires repaired. This was an amazing opportunity to watch the *mzungu* master of local bartering at work. Leon knew what to expect.

As we pulled into a service station, we stopped in the repair area rather than at the fuel pumps. This gave the sharks their first scent of blood. A

---
* Journal entry for Thursday, January 5, 2017.

January 5: First-World Problems

couple of repairmen walked leisurely toward the vehicle. When Leon, a *mzungu* man, stepped out of the vehicle, it was like throwing a bucket of blood in shark-infested waters. People came from everywhere!

The repair work at gas stations in Kenya seems to be—to say it in a nice way—a cooperative effort between the gas-station manager and numerous small-business owners. People came from around the gas station, down the road, across the road, and in the middle of the road. "Leon loves this," Carole said, with her tongue planted firmly in her cheek.

Leon carefully selected one man and began dealing with him. Later Leon explained, "They all want money. Every man who does anything will want to be paid substantially for his small part."

Leon took a flat tire off the back of the vehicle and explained to the man of his choice, "It has a hole in it. Soapy water and plugs are all you need to do. I will give you one hundred and fifty [shillings] for the job."

The man took the wheel, rolled it across the road to his puncture-fixing stand, and began taking the tire off the rim.

"No!" Leon said. "Just the holes!"

Back in the car, Carole said, "We should get some drinks. They might have something in the shop." After a brief search, we found a refrigerator with some Fanta, Coke, and a fruit drink.

As I returned to the Prado with the bottles, I was accosted by a local superhero.

"I am Puncture Man." He pointed seriously at the rear tire and said, "Flat tire."

I agreed that the tire was definitely low.

"I fix now!"

"I am not Boss Man," I said. Pointing across the road at Leon, who was defending the abused tire on the other side of the road, I said, "He is boss man. He decides."

"You talk to him," Puncture Man said, sweeping his cape aside and valiantly stopping traffic to lead me across the road by the arm.

When I arrived at Leon's side, I explained the other tire to him.

"Yes, it will be fixed next," he said.

I said, "This is Puncture Man; he is here to rescue the other tire from certain death and destruction." (I may have said something less witty at the time, but stories get creative in the retelling.)

Leon explained that he only hires one man at a gas station to keep costs in control.

I explained this to Puncture Man, and he was not happy.

"It's faster for two men with two tires," he said.

I pointed sadly at Leon and said, "Boss Man." Then I shrugged my shoulders and raised my palms in front of me.

"So bad," Puncture Man said. "So very bad."

"I'm sorry," I said before I walked back across the busy road, alone and unprotected by any local superheroes.

When the two tires were repaired, the fun really began. The men wanted seven hundred shillings for the three hundred shilling job. Leon explained, before the men began, that the job (which he has had done many times at many places in Kenya) is worth 150 shillings a tire.

Among the many comments that exceeded their language barrier were *"No!"* and "Come off the grass!"

"You will pay each man!"

"I will not."

"You will pay seven hundred!"

"Come off the grass! I will not!"

The ladies in the back seat were giggling uncontrollably. Anyone who knows Leon, loves him for his gentle nature. But as Leon says, "When it comes to God's money, I will not waste it!"

To save money, Leon does most of the repair work on the Prado himself. He has two shock absorbers he will install before we head out of Eldoret on Wednesday for our next long drive. With all the skills to repair the vehicle himself and the knowledge of local prices, highway robbery takes Leon's righteous indignation to unknown heights.

After leaving Kisii, we had driven an hour or so when the Coke and *chapatis* combined in an explosive brew and caused my stomach to begin behaving very disrespectfully. Every jump and jostle sent gases wheezing through my internal pipes in all directions.

After an hour or two of shifting my position repeatedly in an attempt

January 5: First-World Problems

to ease the discomfort, I mentioned my agony to the other passengers. Graciously, no one said they were already aware of my situation.

"We will stop at the next service station." Leon said, "They will have a bathroom."

Sometime later we came into a town and found a service station. We asked about a bathroom, and we were led through a warren of backstreet rooms behind the station.

A woman said, "You want washroom?"

I nodded, and she pointed at a door.

Upon pushing the door open, I knew I was out of luck. I entered and closed the door because I did not want to show disrespect. This was no washroom—there was nowhere to wash anything. There wasn't even a recognizable toilet. Instead, it appeared that someone had installed a urinal by embedding it flat on its back into the floor and concreting around it.

I couldn't begin to imagine how to use it.

I exited, and the next person took his or her turn.

Leon explained how to use the pit toilet to me. "It's not an easy task."

"I'll pass," I said.

"We can look for a Western toilet in the next town," Leon said.

And we did.

In the next town, we stopped at a hotel, and I was led to the back, then outside and around the corner of a building, and shown a brick outhouse. The door, around the backside of the building, was broken off the hinges. Inside, two wooden slats hovered precariously over a pit.

I returned to the Prado for another hour of intestinal disrespect.

As we pulled up to the final gas station, Leon said, "Hopefully, this one will have what you need."

"At this point," I said, "anything will do. This ends now!" As I opened my car door, I said, "Here goes everything."

Laughs of sympathy rippled out of the door behind me.

Four hours after my stomach first announced its unwillingness to comply quietly, I entered the third toilet block. There, gaping up at me, was a concrete version of the first room. Following Leon's advice, I became a world traveler.

The clearest defining line between two sides of the world has been made clear to me: those who use pit toilets and those who do not. While it is not an opportunity I will actively seek out in the future, it is one I can now safely negotiate.

Returning to the vehicle, I was in much better spirits. As we joined the bustling traffic and continued our journey, I felt a new sense of solidarity with the wider world and camaraderie with my three gracious travel companions.

Chapter 20

Nestor's Story

In 1994, eight-year-old Nestor Ndayishimiye and his family were forced to flee their homeland of Rwanda. In the crush of thousands of other genocide-displaced families, Nestor moved along on foot with the momentum of the crowd for hours. When evening came, he could not find his parents.

It wasn't until returning home a year later that Nestor was reunited with his siblings and parents. Nestor's two sisters and four brothers had managed to stay with their parents during the year. Only he had been lost.

"I know what it is like to be an orphan," Nestor said. "I was one for a year. It is very scary and hopeless."

The walk to safety was long and difficult. Many did not have the stamina or strength to survive the stress and loss of becoming a refugee. Some died from the physical exertion. Others died from the torment of reliving, with each step they took, the deaths of their loved ones. "I saw people die as we walked," Nestor said. "People just fell over. There were piles of dead bodies on the road.

"As I walked day after day, I asked God, 'How can I help people so they will not die?'

"My parents were Catholics," Nestor explained. "I was even an altar boy. When I was in high school, I played soccer for my district. The national police team saw me play and recruited me to play for them! Then my parents put me in an Adventist high school. I became an Adventist at the school and combined my love for sports with the Adventist health message."

During his year of living so close to death, Nestor developed a passion for life. His focus on health from that year and through high school shaped him into the person he is today.

"I began teaching health at Adventist churches in Nairobi," Nestor said. "Then I was invited to Kisii to teach in churches in the area. From there, I was invited to Eldoret to teach about healthy living."

While running health camps in Eldoret, Nestor taught some street children. "One of them asked me if I could help them go to school," Nestor said. "I didn't know anything about schooling in Kenya, so I started asking around."

During the next two years, Nestor founded a program called Hands of Hope East Africa, which is now a registered community-based organization in Kenya. With the help of some local and overseas friends, Nestor was able to place some street children in a nearby Christian school. There they were safe, well-fed, and educated by caring teachers.

"Then one day," Nestor explained, "I met Colin Hone from Holy Spirit Ministries. He had come to Eldoret from Australia to run the Ten Days of Prayer meetings. We ran his program for the pastors in three areas. In time, I became the director of Holy Spirit Ministries in the East Africa region. I took the health training and Holy Spirit Ministries around to many churches."

Nestor handled the book sales and finances for Holy Spirit Ministries honestly and efficiently. After Colin Hone returned to Australia, he recommended Nestor to Carole as someone who shared her vision of educating and caring for children who were desperately in need of help.

For a time, Carole and Leon had been involved with an Australian association that supported a children's home in western Kenya. Due to corruption and financial mismanagement by the staff in Kenya, the program had had to be shut down. Carole, motivated by grave concerns for the welfare of some of the children and an obligation to the people who had faithfully supported them over the years, sought the help of a close friend in Kenya. Together they were able to arrange for those children to be accepted into Nestor's Hands of Hope East Africa program.

"This was a huge relief to me," said Carole, "as I knew that Nestor could be trusted and that the children were in very safe hands."

Nestor managed the payment of the school fees, and every cent of money was accounted for. Some of the students from the former children's home were attending various high schools, and Nestor allowed them to spend their vacations with him and his children.

This was another relief, as rape of girls and early teenage pregnancy are very common; but in Nestor's program, the girls are safe during their holidays.

At the end of 2015, the owners of the Christian school decided to close the school down, leaving the children with no school to attend. Soon Education Care Projects—Kenya was able to rent a disused school building for Nestor to move his program to.

"We named it Hands of Hope Academy and began filling it with children," Nestor said. "In the past two years, we have grown to sixty-three students. The school building is not ideal but was affordable and available; and for that, we are grateful.

"Hands of Hope Academy is a place where the children can be free to be educated and live a biblically healthy lifestyle. When we started the school, we brought the fifty-four sponsor children we had placed in other schools into the new environment and gathered a few new ones from the streets.

"I teach the students both sides of each health choice. I do not demand obedience. I allow decisions to be made. The freedom of choice is very important. Many people here in Kenya like my message because I do not point my finger and demand obedience. I give them a positive alternative and let them choose."

At Hands of Hope Academy, children are taught the health message and are given healthy options and the freedom to choose. "About half the students are vegetarians now. All of them live a chemical-free lifestyle—free from drugs, alcohol, and caffeine," Nestor said. "They have gardening responsibilities and plenty of room for sports and play.

"We are raising them in as close to the ideal Adventist home as we can get in a school setting. Last year thirty-two students were baptized!

"We don't push the children," Nestor said. "As the director, I could do that. But when they become adults, they will go back (to previous choices). When they make the decisions for themselves, they are more likely to be permanent. That's how we do it here."

Chapter 21

January 6:
Hands of Hope Academy

We arrived at the Adventist Guest House in Eldoret late Wednesday night after a full day of travel.* I carried my luggage into my room and took a shower. While it wasn't as nice as showering at home, it was water falling from above, and it was a beautiful experience!

I slept well and enjoyed a second shower in the morning. The showers use an instant-heat mechanism that you must switch on before entering the shower. After waiting for it to kick in, you turn on the single knob and find the sweet spot where cold and warm are equalized to your liking.

Oddly, the shower is above the toilet. The one room serves as shower, toilet, and sink. During a shower, the toilet is completely soaked as is the entire tiled floor of the bathroom. This leads to slippery moments and a constant mental reminder to check the floor before entering the bathroom later as it will likely be as slippery as a wet fish.

After showering, I put my dirty clothes together and took them to the housekeeping people. For a small fee, they washed, dried, ironed, and folded my muddied clothes. This was a true blessing!

In the dining hall at breakfast, Amos came to visit. Amos had been a student at the children's home Carole had visited in 2007. Carole and Leon had not seen him in four years, and it was a joyous reunion. Amos had done well at his university, studying for a degree in mathematics. His

---

* Journal entry for Friday, January 6, 2017.

Mary is one of the five children we visited at home in the slums of Eldoret and offered a sponsored education at Hands of Hope Academy.

aim was to work as a statistician, and he graduated in December 2017 with top marks.

At this time, he needed to find a company where he could complete his internship prior to his graduation, and he noted that he was having some difficulty locating a place that would allow him to do so.

At breakfast the next day, I entered the dining room and introduced myself to the only man in the room. With his laptop in front of him, Hesbon was preparing for a meeting he would have in a few minutes. I asked him what he did for work.

He said, "I work at hospitals all around Kenya."

"Do you see a lot of traumatic injuries?"

"No; I don't work in that part of the hospitals," Hesbon said.

"Oh? What is your work?"

"I am a statistician," he said. "I collect and compare data from our hospitals and help them provide the best service by analyzing the data."

I told him about Amos, and he said, "I have just sent a young man from his internship to Nairobi where he is to start a new job this week!"

January 6: Hands of Hope Academy

"Do you need another intern?" I asked.

"If I do not use him," Hesbon said, "I will arrange for an internship in medical statistics for Amos."

Leon walked in, and I introduced them, giving Leon a quick update. The two men swapped stories and details, and it looked like Amos wouldn't struggle to find an internship.

While we ate our second breakfast, Leon said, "That is a God thing!"

Carole said, "God does things like this for these children over and over. He truly blesses them because they are His special children."

Between those two breakfasts was an amazing morning filled with meeting children and seeing their situations both before and after being taken to Hands of Hope Academy.

First, we drove to the academy and met Nestor, the passionate leader behind all that happens there. Nestor is the administrator and ensures that the students and teachers have what they need to get the best education possible for the children rescued from the Eldoret area.

Margaret has just been told that tomorrow we will return and take her to school at Hands of Hope Academy. She looks anxiously out the door and says, "Today! Today!"

Most of the students at Hands of Hope Academy were living at the local dump before they were rescued, cleaned up, and taken to the boarding school just outside Eldoret. Among the children rescued, only one has left the school and returned to life on the street. The change in the children's lives is enough to keep most focused on a better future through Christian education.

Late last year the students participated in an evangelistic program, and thirty-two of the sixty-three were baptized. This combination of faith in Christ and education gives them the best possible start in life and leads them toward eternal life as well.

The other children at Hands of Hope Academy, like the five we met, came from slum areas around Eldoret. The parents of these children have decided to send their children to the boarding school to provide hope and a future for them outside of the slums.

After visiting the students and sharing a time of worship and games with them, we entered each of Eldoret's three slum areas to meet the families of our five new students. It is hard to describe the poverty and dire need we encountered.

The mother of one child explained to our translator that when the family cannot come up with the two hundred shillings (two US dollars) a week for rent for their slum house, the landlord comes and locks the entire family outside until they give him the money.

I asked the translator how much rent runs in the city, just a few blocks away.

"About seven thousand shillings a month," she said.

To leave the slums, a family must afford nearly ten times more each month for rent than they are already paying. It is an impossible situation. So they continue living in makeshift housing with their livestock and children sharing the same tiny room.

The children we visited in the slums were about seven years old—ready to start school.

First, we met Agnes and her parents. Our translator, Eucabeth, showed the parents photos on her tablet of their son, John, who started at the school a couple of months ago. They looked at the pictures but were not sure it was really him. But as Eucabeth flipped from one photo to the next, they realized the clean boy wearing the school uniform was, indeed, their son. Laughter and tears followed as they showed the pictures to the other children in the room.

The transformation truly is amazing. As I am writing this, the others are outfitting the five new students with clothing and shopping for their needs this term. They will return soon, and we will scrub the kids down and give them fresh haircuts. Then in their new clothes and looking their very best, we will take them to meet their new school friends.

January 6: Hands of Hope Academy

Courtney Tyler with the six children whose parents were offered sponsorship for their child to attend school at Hands of Hope Academy.

The second child we met was Margaret. Excited about going to Hands of Hope Academy, Margaret stood by the open door the entire time we were there. When we explained that tomorrow we would meet her family in the city to shop for school supplies and then we would go to school, she shook her head. She said something, and the translator said, "She says, 'I want to go now!'" We assured her that we truly would take her there tomorrow, and she relented.

The third child we met was Mary. Her mother, a single woman, lives with her sister and struggles to feed her children. Both Mary and her mother were so excited about the opportunity for a new life for Mary.

To reach the final stop, we put the Prado into low gear and crawled up a steep hill to the poorest part of the slums. Turning left and driving down a long walking track, we found a tiny shack made from pieces of corrugated steel siding that housed Sophia, her mom, and many other children.

"Where do they all sleep?" Courtney asked as we walked across the rubbish-strewn ground toward their home.

With her long dreadlocks and intelligent eyes, Sophia was my favorite.

She was dirty from head to toe but exuded beauty and wit. As we talked to her mom and played games with the kids—they love shaking *mzungus*' hands and jumping like rabbits—our final recruit walked up with his mother.

The boy's mentally challenged mother is cared for by the community around her. Through the translator, Collins's mother expressed her joy that we would educate and care for her little boy. Clearly a bright young man, Collins was looking forward to joining the program at Hands of Hope Academy.

Carole just stuck her head into the dining room where I am writing and said, "We are back. We have six, not five!"

Leon had been praying for a certain boy, asking if it was God's will for this one too. "God has put this boy on my heart. We must see what we can do."

Finding these six students among the thousands in the slums of Eldoret was the passion of Eucabeth, who served as our translator there. Eucabeth walked the slums every day and talked to the people. As I walked with her, it became clear that everyone knew her. She exuded the compassion of Christ as she embraced and exchanged greetings with the people.

Most of the students sponsored to attend Hands of Hope Academy were orphans rescued from the Eldoret dump. These children spent their days rummaging for food and doing odd jobs for shop owners to earn enough money to buy glue. They put the glue into bottles and strapped the bottles under their noses. This shoe glue is highly toxic and it gave them a quick and consistent high. It also damaged their brains.

Eucabeth visited the dump regularly and talked to the children. Whenever she finds a new child—one with a fully functioning brain—she calls Nestor at Hands of Hope Academy and says, "I have found a child who is able to go to school. Do you have another place available?"

Without Eucabeth, it would be impossible to find the needles of potential in the jumbled haystack of Eldoret's discarded children.

Chapter 22

Eucabeth's Story

Eucabeth Owino has a God-given passion for helping poor people in Eldoret, Kenya.

"I love people!" Eucabeth says. "I walk in all these areas. I talk to people in the slums. I visit the street kids in the fields."

When she returns from visiting the slums and dump with information about people who need immediate help, Eucabeth connects them to the organizations that can provide for their needs. "I check to see that it is safe for other people to go out there," she said.

Eucabeth runs a clothing business in Eldoret. She uses this as a base from which to connect the two worlds in her city—those who need, and those who provide.

Eucabeth explained, "While my marriage was falling apart, I wanted to die. I tried to die. But God would not let me die.

"One night I dreamed about street children. They were brought to me in my dreams."

When she woke, Eucabeth decided it was just a dream. Then she had the dream again the next night and the next.

"For two years," Eucabeth said sadly, "I refused to help them. Then one night in my dreams, God said, 'You died two years ago. I gave you your life back. Now it's time for you to live for Me. Go and give life back to these children!'"

Eucabeth has now worked with the street children for four years. "I do spiritual counseling. I tell them what God says they should do and what He says they should not do!"

"Sounds like parenting," I replied.

Eucabeth walks the slums and dump in Eldoret searching for children whose minds haven't been ruined by sniffing glue. She then recommends them to Carole and Leon for education at Hands of Hope Academy.

"Yes!" she laughed. "They all call me Mother. They appreciate someone telling them the truth."

Eucabeth connects the children she meets with several organizations. One of these organizations is Hands of Hope Academy. When she finds a child who seems like a promising student, she calls Nestor; and once there is means, Nestor arranges a rescue (for the orphans) or a recruitment (for the children with families). Then the child begins the process of Christian education.

"Some children are on the street," Eucabeth said. "I take them home. This is my reconciliation work. I reconnect them with their parents and make sure they do the right thing. If they have a home, they need to live there, not the dump. But other kids have no place to go. They really suffer.

"The street children who have no hope without help, I organize people to teach them skills. Some are very good at sports; some music, drawing, or painting. These abilities give them skills for life and the hope of a better future."

Eucabeth is a living, breathing example of Christian ministry. Just as Jesus walked and talked with the poor and shared His life with the destitute and healed them one by one, Eucabeth is changing the world one child at a time.

Oh, that the world had more people like Eucabeth—more like Jesus!

Chapter 23

January 7:
Sabbath at Hands of Hope Academy

Sabbath at Hands of Hope Academy was a very full day.* After picking Eucabeth up in the city and driving thirty minutes to the school, we arrived at 10:30 A.M. The children were already singing in one of the classrooms.

We joined them and listened to their beautiful music. They have songbooks in English and have learned many songs I am familiar with. Courtney commented that they have changed many of the tunes. They have adapted the Western hymns and choruses to suit their style and rhythm. We enjoyed hearing the variety and creativity in these new tunes.

After a few songs, a teacher named Kelvin invited me to come into the adjacent classroom with a group of students, the platform party for the church service. We planned who would do which part of the service and then we returned to the worship room.

The church service was a typical one—but with extra singing. When it was time for the sermon, we explored Luke 15 together. I told them that every time God finds one of His lost children, He throws a party. It is so amazing how the three stories of lost things in Luke 15 speak to these children.

Losing a sheep is a very real danger. During the testimony time, one boy shared about how he had to count the sheep every night and that if they were not all in the pen, he would receive a beating.

---
* Journal entry for Saturday, January 7, 2017.

January 7: Sabbath at Hands of Hope Academy

The next story, the lost coin, is very meaningful to those to whom a twenty-shilling coin stands between starvation and their next meal. Losing a coin is a desperate situation, especially with these orphaned children's backgrounds.

Finally, to an orphan, the story of the lost son embraced by the father is a powerful desire in each of their hearts. I assured them that their Father in heaven loves them very much and that when He returns, He will hug each of them. Then there will be an amazing party with the longest table and more food than they have ever seen. We finished with prayer and then sang more songs.

During the afternoon, we had lunch—rice and beans—and a time of testimonies in which several children told their stories. It was a moving time, filled with tears of remembrance and thanks to the sponsors and school for the lives they have now.

Christianity really has skin on it here in Kenya. There are so many people making a difference in the lives of orphans and widows. It's like seeing the stories of Jesus coming to life all around you.

After a testimony time, we walked out to the garden plot where the school grows some of its food. It was a leisurely and lengthy walk through Kenyan bush and past numerous houses made from mud and sticks. As we walked, kids took turns holding my hands. When we stopped, I was asked many questions. My favorite was, "Why don't you *mzungus* shave your heads like normal people?"

I spent time telling the children stories about living in Australia and America.

They stroked the hair on my arms and slapped my hands to watch them turn red. They asked me to lean down so that they could feel my hair.

"It is so soft!" they said. "Do your children have the same hair as you? Can you show us pictures?"

They played a game of flipping through photos on my phone and showing it to a circle of kids eagerly waiting to see the next *mzungu* teenager.

I learned some Swahili as well. I can now point at my nose, teeth, ears, and eyes and say the Swahili word for each.

Many of the kids speak passable English, as they learn it in school. The older the student, the more likely they are to understand most of what I say.

When we arrived back from the walk, we began making dinner—*ugali* (cornmeal porridge) and cooked cabbage. One of the teachers cooked soy meat in a beautiful sauce for the *mzungus*. It was delicious.

Finally, at almost 9:00 P.M., we headed back to town, dropped Eucabeth off at her home, drove to the Adventist Guest House, and fell into bed exhausted but fulfilled just after 10:00 P.M.

Chapter 24

Sabbath Testimonies

One Sabbath afternoon at Hands of Hope Academy we sat outside in the shaded quadrangle between the buildings and shared stories from our lives. After Leon started the ball rolling with his own testimony, a few of the oldest students told their life's journey from lost to found.

Leon's story
Leon started with the story of why he decided long ago to follow God's leading. When his daughter Karyn was just seventeen months old, Leon rushed out to the car to make it to a meeting on time. When he arrived at the meeting, a lady at the venue came running out to the car. She pointed at the space between the car and the trailer it was towing. "Do you know your daughter is on the back of the car?"

Leon said, "It is impossible that a seventeen-month-old child could stay in place on the metal frame between a car and trailer at those speeds and conditions. We were saved from a horrendous tragedy that day."

Leon continued, telling of the beginning of Carole's work in Kenya. Nine years ago, the first time Carole went to Kenya, she went with friends, and Leon stayed home.

"I didn't feel God's call for me to go to Kenya," Leon said.

Three years after that trip, Leon journeyed to Kenya with Carole, wanting to support her, but he hadn't made it his passion. He explained that a year after that trip, "I was at a men's conference with a friend. During the break, we were standing next to each other at the mirror in the bathroom. He looked at me in the mirror and said words that changed my life."

Leon paused and continued quietly, quoting his friend. "You're unequally yoked with your wife, Leon. You know that, don't you?"

Leon says it was at that moment that the call came loudly from the Lord, "Join with your wife. Make her mission yours as well."

"The devil has put many problems in our way," Leon said. "Each roadblock just firms my resolve that we are doing the Lord's work! I am convinced I must serve the poor children in Kenya, and I will keep doing this no matter what the devil does to try to stop us."

His story finished, Leon invited others to share their stories.

Kevin's story

A young man named Kevin came forward and shared his story. Kevin's father had two wives who did not get along. One day Kevin's mother and the other wife got into a fight. Kevin's mother, in a fit of rage, murdered the other wife. This resulted in life imprisonment for Kevin's mother and in his father abandoning him.

Kevin's aunt looked after him until he was two years old, and when she decided she didn't want him anymore, some neighbors agreed to care for him. After a while, the other neighbor said that Kevin would bring a curse on their community, so he was driven away. Kevin was forced to wander the streets and lived with the many homeless children in Eldoret. When he met Eucabeth, she asked him if he wanted to go to school. Kevin was rescued from the streets in April 2016 and is now enrolled at Hands of Hope Academy.

Kevin finished his testimony by thanking his Hands of Hope Academy teachers and Education Care Projects—Kenya in Australia for saving his life and making it possible for him to be safe and have an education.

Francis's story

Francis was born under a cloud of confusion. The man married to his mother said, "Where did you get that baby?"

Believing Francis wasn't his, he threw her out.

They lived in various places as his mother followed work to support him and his sister. After another unsuccessful marriage, the poverty became too much for her, and she moved onto the street. An aunt looked after Francis and his sister.

Francis knew where his mother slept and went to find her one day, as she had been sick. He found her blanket, but she was not in it. When he told his sister, she responded, "Yes, Mother left us today. She died."

Francis, then ten years old, became a street child himself. He went into care homes and back to the street numerous times. During this period, his leg was broken when a car hit him, he had dental trouble, and he started using drugs.

One day Eucabeth took Francis and three of his street friends to see Nestor. Nestor enrolled the three friends in school, but Francis was sent back to the street. Nestor challenged Francis to make better decisions so that next time he would be ready to settle down and go to school.

Sometime later, Francis was arrested, and Eucabeth called Nestor. This time Nestor was convinced Francis would take school seriously. A sponsorship was available, and Francis was taken to Hands of Hope Academy.

Francis concluded his testimony by thanking God and saying when he has graduated and is making money he will sponsor kids like himself to come to Hands of Hope Academy.

Judith's story

"I faced many challenges before I came here," Judith said. "When my parents died, I lived with my older sister." Her sister went out looking for work all day and often didn't come home until very late. "I had to find food for the other children," said Judith.

Judith wasn't able to go to school when she was old enough because she was too busy surviving. "When I asked to go to school, my sister would not allow it," Judith said.

"Bigger kids would abuse me, and I would cry, because I knew if Mom was still here, she would protect me," Judith stated. Finally, Eucabeth convinced Judith's sister to allow her to be educated, and she was brought to Nestor and enrolled in Hands of Hope Academy.

Judith finished her testimony by thanking the school and her sponsors and then saying, "When I graduate and have a job, I want to help my sisters."

Judith graduated from Hands of Hope Academy in 2016 and passed the entry exam to go to high school. She would leave for high school on Monday morning.

Marion's story
Marion's parents died when she was in the third grade. She moved in with her aunt, but her aunt was very sick. In a short time, she was living on the streets with friends. She tried to continue going to school as a street kid but failed her high school entrance exams.

Marion spent many years living on the streets, begging for money and sleeping outside. She would occasionally go back to her aunt's house, but she always ended up back on the street.

Marion said, "When I met Eucabeth, she told me, 'Don't roam around town. You need a home.'"

When Eucabeth took Marion to meet Nestor, he said, "If you want to pass school, you will need to repeat grades."

She said she was willing to do that.

In 2015, Marion started the fifth grade. She is now in the seventh grade and hopes to successfully pass her high school entrance exam after the eighth grade next year.

Marion finished her testimony by saying, "The life I left was horrible. There were no rules and no future. I would like to thank everyone at the school and my sponsors."

Morris's story
Morris ran away when he was abused by his stepmom. He was welcomed by street boys and began a life of crime at a very young age. They walked from town to town, stealing from people.

"Once," Morris said, "my friends stole from some people and were chased, caught, and beaten to death. I was so scared I ran away to Nairobi." He was arrested in Nairobi and put in juvenile detention for three years. Then the court sent him home.

"They gave me a thousand shillings [ten US dollars] and told me to go home!" Morris stated. He went to Eldoret and was put in jail for criminal activity. He was a street thief, drug user, and a drug dealer. He tried to sell drugs in the wrong area and, as punishment, was beaten and molested by the criminals who ran that area of town. He was taken to a hospital in Nairobi.

After getting out of the hospital, he traveled across the border to Tanzania and joined a crime gang. When one of his friends was beaten, he went back to Kenya. He made his way to Eldoret and was arrested again when a friend introduced him to Nestor.

He said, "Nestor asked me, 'What would you do at school?' I replied that I would study."

Morris was just twelve years old when he started at Hands of Hope Academy. Three years later, he's in the sixth grade and is doing very well.

Morris finished his testimony by thanking everyone for giving him a chance to change his life.

Jeremiah's story
Jeremiah spent most of his young life avoiding school. He would make his parents believe he was going to school and then would go to town instead. Finally, he got so tired of being forced to go to school that he ran away from home.

Jeremiah walked to Eldoret and lived on the streets. A local school rescued him, and he stayed for two weeks before running back to the streets.

When Eucabeth found Jeremiah, she told him to meet her at a church the next day if he wanted to change his life. He came, and she prayed for him inside the church. Eucabeth then asked him if he wanted to take education seriously. He said yes and was taken to Nestor.

Jeremiah has been at Hands of Hope Academy for five years and is doing better each year. He finished his testimony by thanking the school and sponsors for helping him.

Silas's story
Silas and his sister were treated like slaves by their family. Silas was forced by his grandparents to look after their sheep instead of going to school and was caned if he didn't please them. His sister ran away when she was

accused of something. Silas was sent to his mother, and she forced him to work, preparing vegetables to be sold by street vendors. Finally, Silas ran away as well.

After living on the streets, Silas went home. He was sent from his grandparents to his mother to his brother and back and forth. He met some friends who were stealing money from people. They made him work for them.

When Silas finally met Eucabeth, he was more than eager to go to school. He was brought to Nestor and enrolled in Hands of Hope Academy where he is thriving.

Silas finished his testimony by saying, "Thank you, Nestor and sponsors, for saving my life!"

Chapter 25

January 8:
Sunday in Eldoret

On Sunday, I stayed at the Adventist Guest House, and my work came to me.* I worked with Pastor Abigail Gichaba, the Children's Ministries director for the Greater Rift Valley Conference, to put together a special day of training for her regional Children's Ministries leaders.

When I went to breakfast at the Adventist Guest House, I noticed a flurry of busyness in the hall where the meetings were to occur. I popped my head in and said, "Wow, this looks great! What's happening in here today?"

I was told there was to be a wedding.

"Have you ever seen an African wedding?" one of the florists asked.

I told her, "Yes, on television."

She laughed.

I went to the front desk and inquired about today's venue for the Children's Ministries training. A few minutes later the receptionist brought me a piece of paper with the name of a church on the other side of Eldoret where the meeting was happening.

By this time, Leon was with me, and he called Carole in their hotel room to get more details. Pastor Gichaba had said it would be here at the Adventist Guest House. Carole came to the dining room and gave me Pastor Gichaba's business card. I rang the number, and she said, "I am just driving into the compound. I will see you shortly."

---

* Journal entry for Sunday, January 8, 2107.

When Pastor Abigail walked in, she listened to the story of our dilemma and said, "I am here now; everything will be fine!"

As she walked out of the dining room to arrange things, I looked at Leon and said, "Now that's leadership!"

He laughed and said, "Especially in Africa."

TIA ("This is Africa") is a phrase used by locals and travelers alike to describe the anything-can-happen attitude and reality of the African people. Pastor Abigail was right. Not only was everything fine, it was amazing. She arranged the most beautiful setting imaginable—outside, under big tents, on a mild, sunny day with a gentle breeze. Pure magic.

Pastor Abigail and I shared the teaching load and presented material on Sabbath School, GraceLink curriculum, Vacation Bible School, children's choirs, and storytelling. The theme for the day was TCI—total child involvement. TCI is Pastor Abigail's Children's Ministries mission for the churches in this conference.

Nearly one hundred people listened as we spoke. My words were repeated by a translator for those who did not understand English. It is always fun working with a translator when the audience consists of adults. They help the translator with words the translator struggles with—and sometimes with words the translator did just fine with too. Then a discussion ensues as to the correct word. It certainly keeps people listening!

Pastor Abigail started the day with introductions and then I presented the worship service: my favorite sermon, "A Telling Theology," that demonstrates that both children's ministries and storytelling are at the heart of the end-time mission of God's people.

The next segment I presented was about building and telling stories that teach a key point. In the next section, I taught how to plan and present a narrative sermon, a storytelling format that keeps people listening for the entire time. My concluding section was on Sabbath School. I taught the four purposes of Sabbath School, and I demonstrated a workshop that leaders can run in their churches.

The full day finished with a photo session in which nearly every participant wanted a selfie with the *mzungu*. I'm glad I wore my new Maasai shirt. It was well received by the guests and made me look the part in the photos!

January 8: Sunday in Eldoret

While I was participating with the Greater Rift Valley Conference Children's Ministries Training Day, the rest of the team from Education Care Projects—Kenya were out at Hands of Hope Academy. Courtney ran a special program for the older girls looking at womanhood, addressing things women face (value and worth, relationships). Leon ran a program for the older boys called "Valiant Men," in which they explored what it means to be men of God.

Carole hosted a beautiful experience for the new families. A *matatu* (bus) was sent to pick up the parents, and they were brought to the school to spend a day seeing the new environment where their children were being educated.

Each parent of the six new students came, and they sat together on the edge of a grassy area where the children played. They greeted their children and watched with joy as their little ones played games with other students. Carole told me it was a beautiful experience, and the parents showed their appreciation many times during the day.

These six children are the first group Hands of Hope Academy has actively recruited from homes in the slums. All the other students have been rescued from the local dump where children survive by eating rubbish and sniffing toxic shoe glue to numb the pain. A few children have also been brought by parents, and a small handful are local kids who live around the school and walk in each day.

It was important to Leon and Carole that the families of these new children understand they are always welcome at Hands of Hope Academy and that their family is still intact. Their children are being educated to bring a better life to their families, not taken away from them.

I was very moved by this gesture. I spend my working life with children as an elementary-school chaplain. Every day my goal is to empower children to return home and honor their parents through compassion and cooperation. To see these Kenyan children separated from their families was very hard for me as it goes against my daily practice.

The integration of the family into the Hands of Hope Academy experience is exactly what my aching soul needed for these families. I, too, went to boarding school and know that it can separate or strengthen families depending on how the school and the parents interact. I believe Hands of Hope Academy is on a very healthy track. They are rebuilding broken lives through love, community, education, and healthy living.

Chapter 26

So Many Stories

This trip to Kenya provided me with more stories in three weeks of experience and listening than I had collected in the previous ten years.

After spending almost a week in Eldoret, visiting Hands of Hope Academy each day, we headed into safari country. I was very excited! I have always loved Africa's animals and longed to see them in the wild. We were going to Maasai Mara, the national park that becomes the Serengeti when it crosses the border into Tanzania.

Driving to Mara West, where we would be staying in Narok County, took a full day. Even though the trip was under two hundred miles, the many bends in the road and people walking along the road slowed us down. And that was only the first 125 miles. The final fifty took nearly half the day—a dirt road with potholes the size of small cars. Weaving around them or navigating through their depths was a series of quick decisions that slowed us down to just a few kilometers an hour.

We arrived just before dark and were shown to our beautiful tents. The camp host generously upgraded us to tent cabins. They were luxurious, with running water, power, and hot showers! The water was heated by a fire under a boiler shared between two cabins.

As we slept, zebras, baboons, and giraffes wandered through our camp. The next morning we got up early and boarded our safari vehicle: a four-wheel-drive with seats rising up out of the back and a tarped roof over our heads. It was brilliant! Courtney and I spent the next two days taking pictures and posting them online. It was a once-in-a-lifetime experience!

On those two days of safari, we saw all the big five: lions, elephants, buffalo, leopards, and rhinoceroses. We also saw giraffes, cheetahs, mongooses, baboons, crocodiles, hyenas, and more.

One adventure turned into a deep and meaningful conversation. After we watched as a young, male lion stalked and failed to catch a topi, we followed him to a distant waterhole. The guide realized a herd of wildebeest was coming to drink and parked in a prime viewing spot.

"You are going to see a kill," our guide said. "I promise you!"

But as we watched the lion hunker down above the water hole and the wildebeest approach from the other side, a belligerent water buffalo stormed out of the water and drove the lion away.

Moments later, the dejected lion walked right past our safari vehicle, just a few yards away from us.

Courtney and Carole started discussing the Holy Spirit.

"The Holy Spirit is just like that water buffalo," Courtney said. "He sees the devil stalking us and drives evil away, sometimes before we even see it coming."

"And He knew I didn't want to see anything die!" Carole added.

And that got me thinking, brooding silently, about all we had seen in Kenya. What about when it doesn't happen that way?

We had seen a lot of this in Kenya—horrible things happening to innocent people and to children. Joseph and Nestor reach into the darkness where these children live and offer them a pathway that leads to the Light. But what about the others?

I heard story after story about girls as young as nine years old taken away from their village and forced to undergo circumcision in preparation for marriage. While it is illegal in Africa, this is an age-old tradition that has moved underground in many communities.

I heard stories of boys who were unwanted, beaten by their fathers, grandfathers, and other men in their lives, who fled—boys who were driven by desperation into a life of crime and gang activity.

I heard so many stories, more than I can recount in this book. There are some that I haven't told in detail because the content is too shocking. Others I haven't told because the story is yet another retelling of one already told in these pages. Rael, Christine, Dorcas, Duncan, Grace, Mary—each story, told or untold, represents a broken child.

So Many Stories

Carole Platt stands looking over the village and surrounding area of Kapune. This place and its people have stolen Carole and Leon's hearts. There are always more children to bring to safety.

Hearing the stories of others empowers us to make a difference. By hearing, we are called to care. By caring, we are called to action. And in action, we begin to change lives.

But facing these stories can leave your soul numb. Overwhelmed by the cast of broken characters a million children deep, we begin to wonder, Can I really make a difference? We lift our eyes to the horizon and see an impossible number of children in need of rescue. And we question our own sanity and effort.

Yet wisdom's answer calls us to act on behalf of the one, rather than in some misguided belief that we must change the many for our actions to matter. Each act of kindness matters in many ways. It matters to the one we help, changing his or her life. It matters to us, reinforcing our own convictions within our hearts. And it matters to those who hear our stories, inviting them to become people who care enough to join people who make a difference—people who save the world one child at a time.

Something happens to your heart when you recognize yourself in those you are saving. Hearing your own name in the life of another, and you are humbled.

One day in Kapune, Carole, Courtney, and I were having lunch when there was a knock on the door.

It was Joseph. "Lekini and his uncle are here to see Carole." (You can read the rest of Lekini's story in chapter 18.)

There is just one bit of the story I left out until now because it has been a redefining story in my life.

We listened to the story of seven men who had tried to hack Lekini and his brother to death but didn't realize Lekini was still alive despite the odds. We saw the scars: a huge cut across his forearm and angry scars across the top, side, and back of his skull. Lekini had lived through hell. And now he was going to a Christian school to become, he hoped, a lawyer.

"You need to choose an English name," Carole said to the uncle through Joseph's interpretation skills. "The school requires it."

Lekini and his uncle had been present for the morning meeting. I had talked about God's love for us. Lekini's uncle looked at me, and his eyes filled with tears.

"David," Joseph said. "He wishes that Lekini be called David so that one day he may speak of God as you did today." Joseph paused as my eyes filled with tears. "This is a great honor," Joseph said.

I nodded my head and said, "I'm happy for Lekini to have my name."

It mattered to that one. Every orphan in Africa—each child saved by Joseph and Nestor—is another Lekini. Another David. Another me. It matters to this one.

The conversation about the water hole continued a couple of days later. The safari was finished, we were in the car on our way to Nairobi, and we had a long drive with plenty of time to talk.

Carole voiced what we had thought many times over the past few weeks: "If the devil is defeated at the Cross, why are there still such horrible things happening?"

Carole and I were riding in the back of the Land Cruiser, where we were able to have a deep conversation. "God's followers have a habit of getting things wrong," I said. "Jesus' disciples misread the prophets and were looking for a deliverer who would rule with an iron rod—a warrior-king. Today we've been sold a wrong idea about God, and we tell it to our children.

We tell them that God's defining attribute is power. If this is true, then all that happens on Earth is ultimately God's fault because God is in control. He controls everything with His divine power. This is not God's wish, not the way He wants to be seen or the way He actually is."

Carole said, "God is love. Love—I know that is God's main characteristic. But doesn't love save those who suffer?"

"Within the bounds of God's perfect love, His power lives," I said. "But the ultimate revelation of God's love is freedom. The perfect love of God allows choices to be made and then He honors those choices. But ultimately, love will win. God's love is perfect. It is patient, long-suffering."

Jesus demonstrated that God is love. The apostles, taught by Jesus, repeated that God is love. It is the love of God that compels the hearts and minds of true believers in every generation. And that love is seen most clearly in the death and resurrection of Jesus. That's how God demonstrates His love and frames His power.

Jesus came to this earth to demonstrate the love of God. He came to our water hole, so to speak. Before Jesus took the cross of Calvary upon Himself, His disciples had the wrong idea about His mission.

When the disciples came to the water hole with Jesus, they knew Him well, and they knew the powers that stood against Him. They knew about the devil and his angels. They knew about the water hole's lions and crocodiles. But they thought Jesus' power would dominate. They thought the Messiah, the Warrior-King, would walk unscathed through this world. Like an elephant at the water hole, Jesus would be untouchable, and He would set up His kingdom.

And so, they looked for power in the life of Jesus, and they saw it! But what they didn't realize is that Jesus' power is confined within a greater reality—God's love. They watched what they thought was an elephant walking through the streets of Jerusalem and wondered how anyone could miss it! They asked, "When? When will Jesus demonstrate His power?"

They were looking for the wrong animal at the water hole. Jesus hadn't come to show power but love. He hadn't come to fulfill the wishes of the disciples but to reveal the nature of His Father. He hadn't come to the water hole as an elephant, stomping His way to victory. He hadn't come as a water buffalo, sniffing out evil and driving it away.

Jesus said, "If you've seen Me, you've seen the Father." He hadn't come to show God's power but God's love.

Jesus showed God's love by entering this world as a human. Like many others before Him, Jesus was lifted up and nailed to a cross. Rome had crucified thousands. Jesus entered our water hole like any of the millions before Him. The devil, like a roaring lion looking for someone to devour, leaped upon Jesus, driving his claws into hands and feet.

And Jesus died.

"If you've seen Me," Jesus said, "you've seen the Father" (see John 14:9).

Jesus said, "I give you a new command: Love one another. Just as I have loved you, you are also to love one another. By this everyone will know that you are my disciples, if you love one another" (John 13:34, 35)

After a long drive and discussion on the nature of God and the world, Carole said, "So we just love these kids, and that's enough?"

"Yes," I replied. "But there is something else we give them. You talk about it all the time."

Carole said, "Hope. We give hope to the children we save because we are teaching them about Jesus. That gives them a hope for a future beyond this world of pain and death."

"Yes!"

Carole continued, a bit excited now, "And we are giving them an education that will provide a chance at a happier life than they would have had on this earth. I just wish we could help more, save more, change the lives of more children."

"You are," I said. "And you're doing it God's way."

"We are?" Carole asked.

I said, "Yes. God doesn't see time like we do. Before He rescued the children of Israel, He waited hundreds of years. And due to Israel's stubborn disobedience, the rescue plan took forty years to complete. When changing the lives of many, God works on a generational time scale rather than performing quick fixes."

"How is that like what we are doing?" Carole asked.

"You are educating these kids," I said. "When they are grown and married, they will teach their children what they have learned. You are taking entire families out of poverty. One child becomes one generation becomes, in time, one nation—Kenya. You are changing the world, Carole, in God's way."

There are thousands of children who are like the wildebeest heading to the water hole. It is a rare person who can live among them like Jesus, or Joseph or Nestor. This is a very special calling, but all of us are disciples.

And like the disciple Peter, we are still alive because we have accepted the rescue Jesus offered on the cross and the eternal life He promised by conquering the grave. We have hope because we know the rest of the story. May we make this hope of a better life a reality for as many of God's children as possible.

Chapter 27

When the Lost Is Found

When I returned home from the trip to Kenya, it took me weeks to process what I had experienced. The true meaning of it only became clear the second time I was asked to preach about my trip.

My first sermon at home took place just a few days after my return. I told stories about the trip, stories about the need, and stories about the culture. And I invited people to help.

In preparation for my second sermon a few weeks later, God reminded me about the first night's worship in Kenya. We had arrived in Kapune late in the evening, greeted the children with a touch to the head, and then eaten dinner as darkness overtook the rolling hills of Maasai land. As we finished, Leon told us the children would be arriving soon for worship.

Knowing it was late and that I would be speaking through a translator, I wanted to have a quick, clear message. I had prepared many talks, but nothing seemed right after seeing the environment and the kids.

Leon had been doing the evening worships with the kids, so I asked him what I should say. "What do they need to hear?"

Leon said, "I tell them the same thing every night. I tell them God loves them very much. They hadn't heard this before they came here. We have a lot of catching up to do."

I felt God's Spirit rest upon my spirit, and a message quickly formed in my mind: Luke 15. When God finds someone who is lost, He throws a party because God loves each of us. He loves you and you and you! That's the point of all three stories in Luke 15.

The children filtered in through the entry of our mud hut. Soon the room was full of the sixteen orphan children who had come home for

When the Lost Is Found

Christmas break, Joseph and Mercy, their five children, and the four of us from Australia.

Leon led the children in singing a few songs, prayed, and then introduced me.

"Have you ever lost something?" I asked the kids. A few stories were told by the kids, and then we moved into Jesus telling stories about finding lost things in Luke 15.

A shepherd has a hundred sheep. When he loses one sheep, he puts the other ninety-nine in a pen and goes searching. When he finds the lost one, he picks it up and puts it on his shoulders. He carries it home, puts it in the pen, and then throws a party. He goes from house to house, friend to friend, and says, "I found my lost sheep. Come! Celebrate with me!"

A woman has ten coins. When she loses one of them, she searches the whole house. She sweeps everywhere and finally unearths the coin. She travels from house to house, telling friends and neighbors the story: "I've found a coin that I lost. I'm so happy. I'm throwing a party! Come! Celebrate with me!"

In each story, the percentage of what is lost goes up. In the first story, one in a hundred is lost. In the second story, one in ten is lost. Then Jesus tells a final story about a man with two sons.

The listeners in Jesus' day, hearing these three stories, would have recognized this final story as the main point. This is the big one. It's not a 1 percent loss or a 10 percent loss. It is half; half of everything the father has. The son takes his half, wastes it all—and then, broken and in tears, he makes his way home.

The entire walk home, the son practices his speech: "Father, I've sinned against God and against you. I am no longer worthy to be called your son. Let me be one of your servants!" Over and over, he repeats this to himself until he nears the property of his father.

As I told these stories to the children that first night in the mud hut that would be our home for the next week, I repeated the son practicing his speech three times, "Father, I've sinned against God and against you. I am no longer worthy to be called your son. Let me be one of your servants!"

I wanted the kids to feel the struggle the boy was feeling as he walked toward his father's house. When I repeated it the third time, Joseph looked at me, pausing as if to say, "Do you really want me to translate it all again?"

I nodded.

"The father was standing in front of the house," I said. "And he saw his son while he was still a long way away. And guess what he did? He picked up his stick and ran toward the boy."

Every Maasai boy and man carries a stick. It has many purposes. It is a walking stick. It is a prodding stick for cattle. It is a weapon for defense against predators.

The children went through their mental list of why the father might have picked up his stick.

"The father ran toward his son with a stick," I repeated.

Joseph repeated my words in Maasai.

The kids stared silently at me, wide eyed.

The son saw his father coming. He saw the stick. And he began to yell the speech he had practiced so many times. "Father, I've sinned against God and against you. I am no longer worthy to be called your son."

Before he could finish, his father reached him. He threw his stick to the ground and wrapped his arms around the boy. And then he threw a party! He killed the best cow. And he invited everyone. "My son is home! He was lost, but now he is found. He was dead, but now he is alive! Come! Celebrate with us! My son is alive!"

That's where I finished the story both times I told it to the kids in Kenya, on that first night in Maasai land, and ten days later, on Sabbath when I spoke to the students at Hands of Hope Academy.

"God loves you so much! When He finds you, He throws a party!" I told the kids. "There was a party in heaven the day you were found."

Every child rescued by Joseph in Kapune and Nestor in Eldoret understands the heart of Jesus more than many of us who have not experienced torture, homelessness, or desperation. "You once were lost, but now you're found. God loves you so much!"

For those of us who are more like the Pharisees, Jesus saves the big reveal for the end. The father hasn't lost just one son; he's lost them both— one to the brokenness of those lost in the world and the other to the disconnectedness of those lost in the church. Dead to each other and lost in themselves, neither son understands the love of his father.

While the heart of Luke 15 brings comfort and assurance to those lost and seeking salvation from oppression, the introduction and conclusion of the chapter make it clear that Jesus was aiming at the minds of rich people who were comfortable with their safe lives. They judged Jesus because He spent so much time caring for the poor, broken, and sinful rabble of the world.

"This man welcomes sinners and eats with them."
So he told them this parable (Luke 15:2, 3).

Notice Luke doesn't say, "He told them these parables," even though there are three stories. It was Jesus' intent to present one cohesive message from God to self-focused older brothers. "Celebrate and rejoice, because this brother of yours was dead and is alive again; he was lost and is found" (Luke 15:32).

This disconnect between the brothers is the reason for Jesus' lost-and-found stories. Nothing gives God greater joy than a child being found. Yet amid celebrating the salvation of one, God leaves the party and walks out into the night, where the drums and dancing aren't so loud, to plead with the older sibling. "Please, son, love your brother."

Poverty is, at the heart of it, broken relationships. When God sent His Son to the world, it was to reconnect fallen humanity with the Father in heaven. Before Jesus returned home to His Father, He prayed for you and me, "Father, make them one as we are one" (see John 17:21). Paul also clarified the primary purpose of followers of Jesus as this: making things right with others as God made things right with us.

The older son, standing outside the party, is in the place of the deepest human poverty. Alone, he refuses the will of the father to unite the family of God.

After I returned from Kenya, the meaning of poverty is clearer to me. Poverty exists most where relationships are valued least.

The conflict within me about the meaning of poverty is resolved. It isn't about money. It's about relationships. If all were right between God and the world, poverty would not exist.

I saw some of the richest people in the world while I was in Kenya. Joseph and Mercy are rich. Living in Kapune with their children, parents, orphans, and neighbors as one peaceful, loving community, they have more than we can imagine. The compassionate love and generous forgiveness they have for each other is truly beautiful.

I also saw some of the poorest people in the world while I was in Kenya. From abandoned boys sniffing glue on the streets of Eldoret to eleven-year-old girls circumcised and forced to marry, from children forced to run away because of they were beaten by a grandfather to a politician who "doesn't even have a cow," the poverty of Kenya is in her failing and ravaged relationships.

Because of the call to do as Jesus did, His followers will be caught up in the work of saving God's children for the kingdom. This is done wherever Jesus' followers are modeling Christlike relationships as they rescue the lost.

We can follow Jesus' example by helping those who build relationships both on Earth and in heaven. This is why I value the work of Education Care Projects—Kenya. They are supporting two men, Joseph and Nestor, who are rescuing children from loveless poverty, embracing them with the protecting arms of Jesus, and inviting them into the family of God.